S0-APO-676

# A Comforting Word

*How To Encourage A Grieving Friend*

# A Comforting Word

## Word

*How To Encourage A Grieving Friend*

# KENN FILKINS

KALKASKA
CHURCH OF CHRIST

Copyright © 1994
Kenn Filkins

Printed and Bound in the
United States of America.
All Rights Reserved.

Unless otherwise noted, all Scripture quotations
are the author's own translation.

Library of Congress Catalog Number  94-70202
International Standard Book Number  0-89900-680-9

# Dedication

In memory of Victor Bierschbach,
(October 8th, 1931 — August 24th, 1992)
my father-in-law,
whose life taught me about friendship,
and whose death taught me about grief.

# Acknowledgements

I gratefully acknowledge the help of those who contributed to this book.

My warmest thanks to . . . .

Carol Filkins, my wife, for her constant encouragement, for her meaningful reviews, and for our partnership in life.

Leroy and Cheryl Filkins, my brother and sister-in-law, for reviewing the manuscript, for caring, and for their uplifting excitement about the book.

Delores Buis, my writing friend, for her insights on mourning, dying and grief ministry, and for sharing them with me.

Ron Apple, my friend and Elder at the Gilmore Church, for his insights on syntax, grammar, and phrases, and for his partnership in ministry.

Darlene Buchel, my sister in Christ, for her review of the text, for her cheerful spirit, and for feeding my hawk when I'm away.

My many brothers and sisters in Christ — especially at Gilmore — who upheld me in prayer during the writing of this book.

Those who journeyed through grief before me and stained the trail with their tears.

God's grace and comfort to you all.

# Table of Contents

# Introduction

The goal of this book is not to present a theological treatise on the bodily resurrection of Jesus Christ — which I hold to strongly — nor does this work present simply a theological examination of grief and mourning. This book endeavors to provide practical guidance for those seeking to comfort a grieving friend and who want some insight into the mourner's condition, wants, and struggles.

This book is not intended for someone in the midst of grief, but rather for the griever's friend who seeks to comfort him. If you have a friends or family members who are grieving, this book is for you.

Herein you will not find "canned answers" to the questions mourners ask, but together we will learn about *standing by* those in grief. We will examine why most people become uncomfortable around the grieving and avoid them. Then we will see how others overcame that fear and learned to minister to those who mourn.

In the pages that follow we will journey through the Garden Maze of Grief, and battle with the unanswerable questions that mourners ask. In the Garden Maze we will stumble with them as we encounter the Signposts of grief. We will find that the ministry of *listening* is as powerful as speaking. Stories of the grieving will show us how healing comes through pain. In "Death and the Will of God" we will examine why people suffer and die, and "How can God be good and all-powerful and allow suffering?"

We will share practical ways to comfort the mourning in those tumultuous first hours and days of grief. Then we will learn of the healing effect of a personalized funeral and how friends can help to create a funeral that acknowledges the significance of deceased. Therein we will see the healing power and encouragement of stories.

Far too often comforting ends at the graveside service, so we will examine the necessity and methods of encouraging to the mourning after the funeral. We will close with a discussion of learning to say good-bye — how to prepare others for our death.

The stories that fill these pages are from real people in grief. You will see not only their pain, but their faith and hope. Theirs is a trail we must all follow; grief will one day visit every heart.

On their journey they lit some candles so that as we follow we may see The Light.

## Chapter 1

# Trauma, Grief, and a Kind Word

## What to Say to the Grieving

*Nobody tells you when you get born here
how much you'll come to love it
and how you'll never belong here . . . .[1]*
—Land of My Sojourn,  Rich Mullins

*An anxious heart weighs a man down,
but a kind word cheers him up.[2]*
—Solomon

Trauma changes people. Especially so when the trauma is grief. Once someone has been touched by trauma there is no "going back to normal." We are forever different people. There is no going back to "the way things were" nor the way we were. When, for instance, a lady's husband dies the widow's life is altered forever. Nothing will be *normal* like it was before the trauma of her husband's death.

At those moments of trauma and grief an encouraging friend at one's side brings comfort through a sense of God's presence and a comforting word.

Though grief changes people and relationships between people it *is* bearable and we do learn to live again. We are changed but alive.

On July 27th, my wife's birthday, trauma changed our whole family. Early that morning I went fishing with a friend, then took flowers to Carol's office at noon. When I left her office, I drove home to change for my afternoon appointment with a bereaved family. Once home our youngest son, Andrew, told me that he was riding his bike six miles into town to help his mother at the Senior Meal Site. I said, "Okay, I'll be coming into town in a little while and if I see you laying alongside the road, I'll pick you up."

I meant laying alongside the road because of fatigue; Drew thought I meant getting hit by a car.

Twenty minutes later, as I walked to the van to leave for town, Mack (our oldest son) charged out of the house yelling at me, "Mom called, Andrew was hit by a truck on the way into town! The Emergency team is already there. She'll meet you there. . . ."

Those six miles were the longest drive of my life. I drove down that road, not knowing if Drew would be alive, or if he was paralyzed for life, or in a coma. I felt my mind shutting down and locking up in fear of the worst news. Words cannot fully describe the feeling of driving up on an accident scene and seeing the flashing lights, E.M.T. unit, Fire Department, and the onlookers, when you know it is your son they are caring for. It was a mixture of numbness, panic, and prayer.

When I first walked up to Drew, he laid on his back with E.M.T. personnel at his head and feet. Carol was kneeling at his side. He was conscious and in pain. Maybe the first real pain of his thirteen years. The deep gash in his right thigh was as large as a fist and near his ankle another gash went to the bone. But God was gracious.

If Drew had ridden the small BMX bike instead of his new Mountain bike, he could have easily been killed. Riding on the higher bike he was thrown onto the hood of the truck, bounced off the windshield, then tossed onto the side of the road. The accident was not the fault of the driver — Andrew turned in front of him.

As Carol held his hand and I spoke to him, Drew moaned that his leg hurt. Carol looked up and said, "That man there was the driver of the truck. He is quite upset. You may want to speak with him."

The anxiety was written all over the driver's face as I turned to talk to him. He said he was sorry. I told him Drew would be fine and put my arm around his shoulder as we watched the ambulance pull in to pick Drew up. This may have been helpful to the driver but later I realized that what helped me cope with my trauma was an awareness of another's needs and seeking to help him. Later in the emergency room of the hospital I met with the driver and his wife and prayed with them.

At the hospital we learned that Drew had a broken right tibia (shinbone). He then had a few hours in surgery, five days in the hospital, a hip to toe cast for 10 weeks, then was in a removable knee to toe cast until January of the next year.

This accident changed me. Now I realize the preciousness of each of life's moments and how we must carefully choose the words we speak to those dearest to us. They may become the last words we ever get to say to them.

Drew has a newfound appreciation for the power of automobiles and now knows that teenagers are not as indestructible as they think. He had to deal with the fear of riding a bike near traffic and walking on his injured right leg.

The effect of Drew's accident changed me significantly. I now realize that when we lose a loved one to death the impact is much greater and longer lasting than I had ever known.

I wondered, "If this accident affected me in such a traumatic way, then the trauma must be multiplied several times over when a loved ones suffers an accidental death."

## What Is Grief?

When we think of grief and mourning, we most often think about grief because of the death of a loved one. This is the major area of grief but people mourn for other reasons too.

In his book *Good Grief*, Granger E. Westberg wrote, "We spend a good portion of our lives working diligently to acquire those things that make life rich and meaningful — friends, a wife or husband, children, a home, a job, material comforts, money (let's face it), and security. What happens to us when we lose any of these persons or things which are so important to us?

"Quite naturally we grieve over the loss of anything important. Sometimes, if the loss is great, the very foundations of our life are shaken, and we are thrown into deep despair...."[3]

He goes on to describe the loss and grief associated with divorce, retirement, job change, loss of an arm or leg, eyesight, and many other situations where people grieve.

Grief, then, is the natural and painful struggle to cope with a significant loss, so that we can endure with the pain and learn to live again.

## What Is Comfort?

Comforting the grieving is *not* taking their pain away. Comforting does not mean having all the answers to questions that the mourning pose. It does not mean knowing logical answers to all the "why"s of death. Comforting does not mean we help them forget the lost loved one.

Comforting means we gently stand by them as they go through the stages of grief, learn to deal with the pain, and find that they can live again. We comfort them by listening to all their unanswerable questions and their illogical anger without judging them. We comfort by showing that we remember their loved one. We also comfort by acknowledging the significance of their loss and that their lost one is significant — even years after the loss. This is particularly true of those who lose children — more on that later.

True eternal comfort can only come from the assurance of the resurrection through Jesus Christ. First Corinthians 15 abounds with the implications and affirmation of the resurrection of Christ. I rest in the hope — by "hope" I mean *assurance*, not wishing — of Christ that death is not the end but a doorway to life. Karl Barth wrote that because of what God accomplished through Jesus in a cemetery near Jerusalem, the goal of life is no longer death but resurrection.

In *The Gift of Significance*, Doug Manning shared this insightful parable about death that leads to life.

### The Parable of the Twins

Once upon a time, twin boys were conceived in the same womb. Weeks passed, and the twins developed. As their awareness grew, they laughed for joy: "Isn't it great that we were conceived? Isn't it great to be alive?"

Together, the twins explored their world. When they found their mother's cord that gave them life, they sang for joy: "How great is our mother's love, that she shares her own life with us!"

As weeks stretched into months, the twins noticed how much each was changing. "What does it mean?" asked the one. "It means that our stay in this world is drawing to an end," said the other. "But I don't want to go," said the other one. "I want to stay here always." "We have no choice," said the other. "But maybe there is life after birth!" "But how can there be?" responded the one. "We will shed our life cord, and how is life possible without it? Besides, we have seen evidence that others were here before us, and none of them have returned to tell us there is life after birth. No, this is the end."

And so the one fell into deep despair, saying, "If conception ends in birth, what is the purpose of life in the womb? It's meaningless! Maybe there is no mother after all?" "But there has to be," protested the other. "How else did we get here? How do we remain alive?"

"Have you ever seen our mother?" said the one. "Maybe she lives only in our minds. Maybe we made her up, because the idea made us feel good?"

And so the last days in the womb were filled with deep questioning and fear. Finally, the moment of birth arrived.

When the twins had passed from their world, they opened their eyes and cried for joy. For what they saw exceeded their fondest dreams.[4]

## The Loneliness of Sorrow

Mourning is largely a lonely sport. Most people are not comfortable near people who are grieving. Many people find that they not only lose their loved one to death but they also lose contact with their friends with whom they had shared the most.

Many people avoid those in grief, as C.S. Lewis realized after the death of his wife.

Lewis wrote,

R. [his friend] has been avoiding me for a week. I like best the well-brought-up young men, almost boys, who walk up to me as if I were a dentist, turn very red, get it over, and then edge away to the bar as quickly as they decently can. Perhaps the bereaved ought to be isolated in special settlements like lepers.

To some I'm worse than an embarrassment. I am death's head. Whenever I meet a happily married pair I can feel them both thinking, "One or the other of us must some day be as he is now."[5]

After interviewing hundreds of families I have learned that most families want to talk about their loved one and that sharing those memories can become a catalyst for healing.

In my book, *Comfort Those Who Mourn*, I mention Mike and Jo Jones who lost their son, Pat, in a construction accident caused by a tornado. When I heard about Pat, I drove to Indiana to visit them. They said that their friends would talk to them but avoided mentioning Pat's name. Though speaking of him often brought tears, they *wanted* to talk about their memories of him. Sharing

these stories with others was a release valve for their bot-
tled-up grief.

Mike and Jo shared this advice for friends who want
to comfort a mourning family: don't be afraid to mention the deceased by name — it is on their minds all the
time; ask about details concerning the deceased's life —
your curiosity shows you care; and don't worry about
always saying the "right thing" — your compassion and
concern are comforting.[6]

Doug Manning mentions the reason mourners sometimes lose their friends during times of grief. "If any of
them [friends of the mourners] are asked what happened, they would say, 'He just wallowed in his grief.'
The truth is they went over there the night it happened
and could not figure out what to say. After a time of
agony and discomfort they left, saying, 'We will go now,
but if there is anything we can do just let us know.'

"The experience was so uncomfortable they dreaded
going back. The dread led to delay. The delay led to
guilt. Then they had to get angry with the man to justify
their guilt. The result is the man lost a son and six
friends at the same time."[7]

One of the reasons friends avoid people in grief
results from a desire to avoid death and the topic of
death. It seems ironic that a culture which visualizes so
much real and fictional death through the media and
movies, evades death in real life at all costs. Even if it
costs them friendship. Could it be that death is kept at a
distance because of the television screen? Could it be that
we can control the death we see in the media by changing the channel? Is it because people mourning the death
of a loved one remind us that we are not in control? And
our lack of control over death scares us? That fear keeps
us from participating in some grief rituals that bring healing to our mourning friends and loved ones.

# Our Culture's Response to Death

Hebrews 2:15 says that the "fear of death" held us captive before the resurrection of Jesus broke the power and control of death over our lives.

Our culture's avoidance of death is pictured well in this very short story called "Appointment In Samarra."

### Appointment In Samarra

Many years ago, there was a man in Bathsheba who asked his servant to go to market. His servant he had known many years, and was faithful in service. Though his hair was white, he stood as tall as a young date tree in the autumn, whose leaves are beginning to fall, while the fruit of abundance draws to an end about it.

The servant went to market, and among the throng he saw Death, dressed black and as pale as the moon that grows thin. Death made a gesture, and the servant grew frightened; for, although there were many people in the marketplace, who crowded to buy the things that would bring them joy while they lived, none of them heeded the lonely pair.

And he ran home to his master, and he said, "Master, today I saw Death in the market amid the throng. And he made a threatening gesture to me. Master, I shall make haste and I shall ride like the wind to Samarra, for Samarra is many miles from here, and Death will not find me there."

So the servant rode away to Samarra, and his master was sorely troubled, as is the traveler in the desert who is called to the side of his dying father and his long journey draws to an end. And he went to the market and he sought out Death, whose dress was dark as the sea at night when the fisherman is lost, and his face was as pale as a grave on a frosty night.

And the master said to Death, "Why did you make a threatening gesture at my servant? He has done me good service, and is old in years."

And Death replied, "I made no threatening gesture at your servant. That was a start of surprise. For I saw him this morning in Bathsheba, but this night I was to meet him many miles away in Samarra."[8]

This fear of death creates our uneasiness around those who grieve and robs us of some healing traditions.

## Overcoming the Reluctance and Fear of Comforting the Grieving

"When one member suffers, all the members suffer" (1 Corinthians 12:26).

"Rejoice with them that rejoice; weep with them that weep" (Romans 12:15).

As a minister of the Gospel, dealing with grieving families comes with the profession. Still some situations make me fearful, uncomfortable and make me mourn. Monica was one of those times.

### *Monica — A Christmas Baby*

It was December 27th, my son's birthday, and Micaiah — we call him "Mack" — slept in. Around 9:00 am we prepared to go out for our annual birthday breakfast, when the phone rang and Mack said it was Dave Coker, the local funeral director, and he wanted to talk to me. I knew it was likely about a funeral or a grieving family. So I prepared myself for the news and began reviewing my schedule for the next few days. However, I was not prepared for what he was about to tell me.

"Kenn, I'm in a bind," Dave began as I heard the stress in his voice.

"What is it, Dave?"

"I have a funeral this morning at 11 o'clock and the family just called to say that their minister couldn't preside over the service." Dave paused then continued, "It is a stillborn baby that was born and died on Christmas day. Is there anyway that you can help? It will be at the chapel at the Surrey Cemetery."

"That's not an easy one, but I'll be there," I replied,

21

KALKASKA
CHURCH OF CHRIST

"Meet me there at 10:45 a.m. with all the details about the situation."

"Thanks, Kenn, you don't know how much I appreciate this," Dave said sounding relieved.

I became stressed. This service left me just enough time to take Mack out to breakfast, then to the ski lodge and return to the cemetery for the service.

"What will you say, Dad?" Mack asked, "The baby had no personality or stories for you to talk about."

"I'll talk about the *lack* of memories and that it's the anticipation of 'what might have been' that haunts us most when we lose a child," I replied.

When I met Dave we discussed the difficulty of this service. Doctors had told the couple that this baby would not live. She had a disease which left her with no skull from the top of the forehead back. We both mentioned that it was one of the toughest funerals in which to participate. This mother will always remember the death of her daughter each Christmas as others celebrated the birth of another Child.

It was an intimate gathering in the chapel of the Surrey Cemetery on that bitter cold December day. Monica Renee Osborn's body lay in a small casket as the couple, Kim and Dave, entered the chapel with ten family members. Once they were all seated Dave Coker signaled me to start by a nod of his head.

I whispered a silent prayer then began with remarks about the pain of losing a child.

"It's always painful to lose someone we love. It's difficult to lose an elderly person whom we cherish after they have had a long and eventful life. But it's more difficult to say good-bye to a child because we wonder *what might have been.*

"Frank Deford wrote, 'Elderly people die with achievements and memories. Children die with opportunities and dreams.' Part of what makes our pain so intense is that we wonder what Monica might have been like if things would have been different. We wonder if she may have grown to be a scientist who discovered the cure for cancer, or maybe become the first woman president of the United States. We grieve because of what we do not know and we wonder.

"But we grieve more for what we do know. We do know that if things would have been different, Monica would have grown up in a family where she would have been cherished and loved. We, here, would have seen her first steps and her laughter and her smile. We would have found out if she would have looked like her mother and had the personality of her father. We do know we will miss all these things and that hurts.

"Today, we acknowledge that a chunk has been torn from each of our hearts and the pain will not soon go away. We have experienced a significant loss. Kim carried Monica for months and the bond grew strong. The loss is strong too. Dave watched as Kim grew heavy with Monica's weight and he was drawn to his child in love. . . .

"You who know and love Dave and Kim mourn with them. And the loss is particularly compounded by the date of the event — Christmas day. It is the day when people celebrate. Celebrate the birth of a Child. From this year on, Christmas will have its sad tone too for Kim and Dave as they remember Monica. You, family and friends, will remember too. Next Christmas, and those that follow, are days for you to show your love and compassion for Kim and Dave. They will remember Monica on that day, and they will need you to hug them and whisper in their ear that you remember Monica and this Christmas and that you hurt too.

"Remember Dave and Kim every Christmas, share in the grief by telling them you too remember and hurt for

Monica. When we lose someone we love we don't want to forget her, we want to learn to deal with the pain and learn how to keep on living.

"As a Christian, the only Person Who comforts me on days like today is Jesus. He is the only one who offers the hope that this is not the last day, we will see Monica. Because of the bodily resurrection of Jesus Christ we have the promise from God that this life is not the end. Monica's body is here, but her spirit is with God. Down here we did not get to know Monica's personality but one day because of Christ we can see her; full of life and whole and complete. We'll get to meet her, talk with her, and learn about her — all because of Jesus."

Then I mentioned that we are tempted in two areas "in these days of grief. We are tempted to blame ourselves for what happened to Monica. And we are tempted to blame God for this event. Resist both temptations because . . . ." I concluded with a reading from John 14 and talking about God's love, power and comfort.

Then I asked the family to join me in a circle for prayer and Dave Coker joined us as well. After the prayer for comfort and guidance, the people sat back in their chairs and Dave Coker mentioned that the service had concluded. Dave and Kim were not ready to leave and say good-bye to Monica, so they sat silently. The silence was unsettling to some of the family. Many — especially Kim's sisters — just sat there with tears silently streaming down their cheeks.

Knowing this was an important time for the parents, I wondered how the family and friends might respond. After several minutes one of the men of the family got up from his chair and whispered something to Kim and Dave and began to leave. Within a few minutes everyone else was gone, except for Dave Coker, me, and the parents. Kim cried, and tears ran down her husband's face as he held her.

Again I wondered how many couples who lose a child feel as lonely as this couple *looked* just then. Both the funeral director and I spoke with them for a few minutes before they left. Once they were outside I said, "Dave, I just want to cry."

As we shook hands he said, "I know."

Looking into his eyes, I knew he did.

## More Comfortable With Comforting

Sharing with grieving families is never easy. I pray it never is. But it is easier when we remember a few of the ideas that Monica's story reminded me about:

*The grieving do not expect you to have the answers to unanswerable questions.* There are no pat answers for, "Why is a baby born which cannot live?" Remember, the question is not "why" in the clinical sense — the birth defect is clinically the reason. The question is "Why did God make or let this happen?" They are asking about a greater purpose to this death. This will be covered in greater detail later, but a philosophical lesson is not what the mourning need during their time of grief. They need *compassion.* A good answer may be, "I don't know why this happened. . . . But I care, so I'll stay with you as long as you want."

Grievers do not need platitudes or pat answers. They need passion and perseverance. They need friends who show the compassion and determination to overcome the fears of sharing with a friend.

*Mourners do not expect you to take their pain away.* Whenever we see a friend in pain, we desire to relieve it. Do not try to "cheer them up" with trite talk about sports, weather, politics, or jokes. In grief there is nothing you can say to take the pain away.

*Do not fear talking about their loss or the deceased.* One of the many myths of mourning is that "it hurts to remember." Therefore well-meaning friends will visit with the grieving and not mention the death at all. What we fail to realize is that the grieving *want* to talk about the loss. Mentioning the name of the deceased is not only acceptable but, as we will see later, it is *cherished* by the family.

We fear that talking about the deceased will cause more pain and be counterproductive by forcing them to stay in their grief. The reverse is true. It establishes significance and frees them to move toward other stages of healing.

When we talk about their loss and the deceased, we help them establish the *significance* of their loss and of their loved one. Every person's life is significant. God created him in His image and God loved him — even if he never responded to God's love. And Jesus died for him; a substantial price for a valuable person.

His family loved him, then they lost him. Now you can listen and share with them, as they capsulize his whole life — his joys, defeats, trials, sorrows, victories, relationships, and faith.

As we will see later, sharing of the personal stories of the deceased guides the grieving through some uncharted seas of grief. Some may think that it is deifying the deceased if we talk about them, but that need not be true.

"No relationship is all good or all bad," Manning wrote. "The good needs to be appreciated and the bad needs to be acknowledged with honesty and candor."[9]

For most mourners, verbalizing their memories helps them sort out their feelings. Most express feelings of sorrow, loss, and love. Others deal with feelings of anger toward their loved one who "abandoned them" or at

God for "taking their loved one from them." Widows often share their fear of coping with life without their mate.

*People need for those outside the family to acknowledge that they remember and miss the deceased.* Sometimes we fail to comfort the grieving because we think that grief is a private affair for the family only. We may think that no one else should talk about the deceased unless a family member brings him or her up. In reality the grieving are usually very sensitive to the feelings of others and do not want to impose their predicament onto others. They are often relieved to find a friend who is at ease enough with the topic of death and grief to speak to them.

*Remember the goal of the mourning is not to forget the deceased or the loss.* They want instead to know if they will survive the pain and learn to cope with their loss.

This is a painful and confusing journey as we will see next. . . .

# Chapter 2

# The Healing Power of Pain

## The Process of Grief

*Grief only comes in one size – extra large.*[10]
—Doug Manning

*And there is a time for every event under heaven–*
*A time to give birth, and a time to die;*
*A time to weep, and a time to laugh;*
*A time to mourn, and a time to dance.*
*A time to search, and a time to give up as lost;*
*A time to love, and a time to hate;*[11]
—The Preacher

Someone said that grief is like peeling an onion: it comes off one layer at a time and you cry a lot. But grief is not so linear. It is more of a back and forth adventure.

Diana McKendree writes about the pulsating flow of grief in this way:

> You are standing in an ever-changing Sea of Emotion. The waves may knock you down at times, or they may brush softly against your back. Just as ocean waves never stop completely, the waves of your grief do not disappear, but they do carry the potential to cleanse as they gently wash over you. "Blessed are they that mourn, for they shall be comforted."[12]

## Journey Through a Garden Maze

Grief is not a linear experience, where we begin a journey from pain to pleasure like we walk uptown to the corner store. If grief were a linear experience we could draw a map of its journey and watch for the familiar signposts on the trip, knowing that we will not pass them again, and so we will arrive at our destination. We would also know that if we did see those signposts again that we were lost. That lostness would frighten us.

But grief is not a linear journey from point "A" to point "B" with "the shortest distance between being a straight line." Nor is grief a cycle that revolves or spirals.

Grief is like a journey through a Garden Maze with its tall hedge walls. In gardening, a labyrinth or maze is an intricate network of pathways enclosed by hedges which is difficult to find the center or the exit. The pathway walls are made by parallel walls of yew or holly hedges which are grown too thick to see through. The maze in the gardens at Hampton Court Palace, one of the finest mazes in England, was planted during the reign of William III. The goal of the Hampton Court Maze and others is to reach the center then find your way back out through the same door. The Hampton "key" or map is "go left on entering, then, on the first two occasions when there is an option, go right, but thereafter go left."

For the Garden Maze of Grief the entrance is the death of a loved one. But the Grief Maze differs from the Hampton maze because the exit, The Door of Comfort, is on the opposite side of the Maze. We cannot exit the door we entered because, as we have learned, once grief strikes us there is no turning back. Though there is no map, there are Signposts which tell us where we are inside the maze.

The pain we feel at the death of a loved one forces us into the Maze and we know that we cannot turn back, though we wish we could. As we seek the doorway on the other side of the Maze, the dark clouds of grief keep the sun from sharing any directional insight. We are on our own, except for the Signposts that appear in the

*Layout of the Hampton Court Maze*

Maze to tell us what phase of grief we are encountering.

Inside we find four Signposts: Numbness, Yearning, Despair, and Reconstruction. As we journey toward the Door of Comfort we stumble into these four Signposts seemingly at random, for no two journeys of grief are the same, even for the same person. "Grief is individual as a fingerprint."[13]

As we journey, most of the time we do not know which of the Signposts acknowledges our condition, because we are journeying from one Signpost to another. The journey is not circular because the sequence of our encounter with the Signposts is not the same. The Maze confuses us. But we know from our first time to the Signpost of Reconstruction that the Door of Comfort is nearby. While in the Maze we cannot sit down; our restlessness keeps us moving.

Sometimes we stop at one of the Signposts and refuse to keep trying, because "this familiar pain is better than the unknown one around the next corner." When we stop trying, we become "stuck in grief." We find no comfort.

Finally, if we keep trying, we realize that the dark clouds of grief are moving and the sunlight occasionally begins to peek through the clouds. We begin to get our bearings and find ourselves more often near the Signpost of Reconstruction. We think and feel that we will survive to live again, but not back to our former life. The journey has changed us. We do not mind, however, because we have lost someone important to us. The pain of grief and the Garden Maze have shown us that we cannot be the same.

As observers of those in the Garden Maze of grief, we can be with them on their journey, but we cannot take them by the hand and lead them out. *They must find their own way.*

If we keep trying as time passes, we become more familiar with the Garden Maze and know that we will not be by the painful Signposts forever. We sense that we will reconstruct our lives and find our way out. We learn that there is hope and life outside this Garden Maze called Grief. We hear the voices outside that once were only noises, but now have the alluring, even peaceful, charm of a familiar voice.

As Walsh wrote, "We move, through faith and prayer, between the poles of grief and relief, between the posture of pain and the pleasurable comfort."[14]

Once we are out of the Garden we quickly learn that the we are not the same person who entered the Maze. We now find the Signposts of Numbness, Yearning, Despair, and Reconstruction, outside the Garden, in the midst of life, often when we least expect it. We find that the Signposts of grief are not stationary.

Things never "get back to normal." Grief forever changes us. We banter between the Signposts of grief for months. People often feel that mourners are "wallowing in grief" if they still have intense feelings of loss three months after a death. But mourners are not "stuck on a phase of grief" possibly until after two years.

Grief's Garden Maze is intensely *personal*. Every person, and each time a person grieves, is necessarily different. Our response to death will differ depending on at least three items. It depends first on how we feel about death issues and how our personality deals with trauma. The second is who died and how close we were to them. Grief depends in part on what kind of person we mourn for. Thirdly, our relationship with the deceased determines much about our grief — for a wife in an abusive relationship, her spouse's death may bring a sense of relief. For another widow, her husband's death may mean the loss of her dearest and sweetest friend.

C.S. Lewis described his Garden Maze and its lack of a road map this way:

> Grief is like a long valley, a winding valley where any bend may reveal a totally new landscape. As I've already noted, not every bend does. Sometimes the surprise is the opposite one; you are presented with exactly the same sort of country you thought you had left behind miles ago. That is when you wonder whether the valley isn't a circular trench. But it isn't. There are partial recurrences, but the sequence doesn't repeat.[15]

## The Process of Grief

Because the Signposts of grief are not linear or stationary, anticipating a mourner's journey is impossible. We just know that some time they will arrive at the Signposts. It is the difference between showing someone a map or teaching them to use a compass. Grief is a compass journey.

C. Murray Parkes studies these compass journeys:

> Grief is a process, not a state. Grief is not a set of symptoms which start after a loss and then gradually fade away. It involves a succession of clinical pictures which blend into and replace one another. . . .
> Each of these stages of grieving has its own characteristics and there are considerable differences from one person to another as regards both the duration and the form of each stage. Nevertheless there is a common pattern whose features can be observed without difficulty in nearly every case.[16]

Parkes' discussion of the nature of grief resulted from personal interviews with twenty-two widows at the end of the first, third, sixth, ninth, and thirteenth months after the death of their respective spouses. Parkes describes the four phases of grief as *numbness and denial, yearning, disorganization and despair,* and *reorganization of behavior.*[17]

A COMFORTING WORD

Doug Manning lists the four phases of grief as *Whirl* (a thousand questions run through their heads), *Reality* (the time of the most pain), *Reaction* (the time to fight back or respond, including anger), and *Reconstruction* (people eventually decide to live again).[18]

## Signpost of Numbness and Denial

### *The whirl of a thousand questions*

During the first hours and days of grief we visit the Signpost of Numbness and Denial most often. Parkes' study found that denial lasted anywhere from one day to a month, with five to ten days being the most common. But like the other Signposts of grief, he found that even after a year some of the mourners still found it hard to accept that their loved one was dead.

Denial is the enemy of the grief process. It keeps the process from beginning and continuing. Staying at the Signpost of denial and saying, "I want things to go back to what they were," will have tragic consequences. Coping without presence happens when we begin to find comfort in the memories. If memories don't interest the mourners — they want things back the way they were — they live in and for denial.

A radical example of this is Joanna of Spain. A daughter of Ferdinand and Isabella, she was so distraught by the death of her husband Philip of Hapsburg that she refused to bury him. For years she kept his corpse with her wherever she went, hoping some miracle would restore him to life. Eventually her unremitting grief drove her mad.[19]

Panic is a common symptom at this Signpost. Granger Westberg in *Good Grief* wrote,

When something has been terribly important to us for a

long, long time and it is taken from us, we cannot be expected to do anything but be constantly drawn to the lost object and suffer daily as we struggle with the gradually dawning realization that it is gone forever.

When a person begins worrying about losing his mind, he often panics. He becomes almost paralyzed with fear. It is often fear of the unknown, or fear of something he does not understand, that throws him into this panic.[20]

Finally we begin to see the reality of the loss because too many things confront our denial and we stumble toward the next Signpost. C.S. Lewis shows us his "compass reading" at this phase in the journey.

Tonight all hells of young grief have opened again; the mad words, the bitter resentment, the fluttering in the stomach, the nightmare unreality, the wallowing-in tears. For in grief nothing 'stays put.' One keeps on emerging from a phase, but it always recurs. Round and round. Everything repeats. Am I going in circles, or dare I hope I am on a spiral?

But if a spiral, am I going up or down it?[21]

## Signpost of Yearning

### *Reality of the loss overtakes us*

The second Signpost at which most mourners find themselves is Yearning. They begin to face the reality of the loss and long for the deceased. This phase of grief shows a preoccupation with memories of and an intense longing for the deceased. Much attention is given to the objects and places which remind us most of the deceased. Ten of the widows in Parkes' study thought they had heard or seen their husbands, and sixteen reported a sense of the presence of their husbands near them during the first month after death.

Months after the death of my wife's father and my close friend, Vic Bierschbach, I had a dream that he came to visit us at our home. He had frequently stopped to visit when a delivery for his insulation company brought him into our area. In the dream he sat at our kitchen table drinking his ever-present mug of coffee as we talked about work or fishing. When he got up to leave, it struck me that this was good-bye and I would not see him again. I hugged him and began to cry. Then I awoke. Crying.

That night I realized, I was standing next to the Signpost of Yearning.

Many mourners fall into depression and sadness as a reaction to the reality of the death. It becomes difficult for them to feel enthusiastic about any activity. Their energy level seems too low and they may resent other's encouragement to participate. At times they feel completely out of control of their emotions and think they will never stop crying. The opposite may also be true, as they struggle to understand why they can't cry a single tear. They need to hear that these responses are normal and the dark clouds over the Garden Maze will pass.

Besides depression and sadness another feeling mourners often have at this Signpost is guilt — normal guilt or neurotic guilt.

Normal guilt is feeling sad about something said or done, or some deed left undone or word left unspoken. Neurotic guilt is guilt out of proportion with the reality of the person's involvement with the deceased.

An illustration of neurotic guilt might be a daughter who has stayed by her aged mother's bedside in the hospital for days and days without sleep. The doctor now orders her to go home and get some sleep. This turns out to be the night that her mother dies, and she will never forgive herself for not being there when it happened. She broods endlessly about this and builds it up out of proportion to the real situation. . .We must not be embarrassed to talk about our feelings of guilt with those who can help us when the going gets rough.[22]

Anger often enters the Garden at this Signpost too. Here the grieving person hits bottom, gets mad, and decides to fight back. But anger needs a place to focus. It takes two people to deal with anger, one to speak it and the other to hear it.

Many times the anger is directed irrationally, such as a widow who is mad at her deceased husband for dying of cancer and leaving her alone. She needs to know that these passing feelings of anger are just that, *passing* and normal.

Ministers receive a great deal of misguided anger. Ministers, it seems to me, receive more criticism because of funerals than any other area of their ministry. They are visible and vulnerable targets for those who are angry and needing to direct it somewhere. Much of this criticism comes as a result of impersonal funeral messages. I wrote the book *Comfort Those Who Mourn*, to guide ministers in preparing *personal* funeral messages that substantiate the life of the deceased through details of his or her life.

The grieving often verbally vent anger toward God because someone said that this death was "the will of God." Physicians, funeral directors, family members, and spouses also receive their share of irrational anger.

One place we do not want the mourners to focus their anger is *inward*. Guilt in grief is sometimes anger internalized.

In such circumstances we can later explore those guilt feelings to find their root. With the intensity of emotions at the Signpost of Yearning, it is not yet time for this exploration. There is a time and place outside the Garden Maze. Their immediate need is for comfort and consolation through shared remorse and grief, and not quick answers that could reflect nothing more than our own defensive posture.

# Signpost of Disorganization and Despair

## *Our reaction to the loss*

Once the reality of the loss overwhelms the mourner and they begin to come to grips with it, they find themselves stumbling into the Signpost of Disorganization and Despair.

In this phase of grief the mourner feels a sense of emptiness, a sense that there is no future and that they cannot go on. It is really important, as we will discuss later, that the grieving does not make any long-term, life-changing decisions during this time. In this phase, the intense yearning and sharpness of emotion give way to apathy and aimlessness.

This is the reaction to the reality of the loss. They realize the sinking feeling that this separation will not end and admit that there is no solution to the pain but to endure it. That realization can bring with it the symptoms of depression.

The mourner standing at this Signpost asks, "Why go on?" "Can I go on?" "Can I endure the pain?" and "Can I cope with this loss?"

Doug Manning wrote,

> A couple whose son had accidently hanged himself came to one of my [grief] seminars. We had dinner together and then visited late into the night. All through our time together the woman kept saying, "I just don't want to go on."
>
> When someone says they do not want to go on, the first thing we think of is suicide. When I asked her about suicide, she said there was no way she would do that to her family. The next logical step is to tell her all the reasons she has for going on. When I suggested the reasons she said, "I know I should go on — I know I am going to go on. The problem is I don't want to."[23]

When a mourner gets depressed, he finds himself

thinking thoughts he never would have otherwise. He says God does not care. He may even doubt that there is a God.

> However, the experience of people through the centuries has been that the dark clouds of depression *are* moving; they *do* pass. One of the most helpful things we can do for a friend in such a time is to stand by that friend in quiet confidence, and assure him or her that this, too, shall pass.[24]

C.S. Lewis acknowledges the whirlwind of emotions that sweep the mind off balance during grief. After he questions God's goodness, he writes,

> Why do I make room in my mind for such filth and nonsense? Do I hope that if feeling disguises itself as thought I shall feel less? Aren't all these notes the senseless writhings of a man who won't accept the fact that there is nothing we can do with suffering except to suffer it? Who still thinks there is some device (if only he could find it) which will make pain not to be pain. It doesn't really matter whether you grip the arms of the dentist's chair or let your hands lie in your lap. The drill drills on.[25]

The initial journey between the Signpost of Despair and Reconstruction begins when the grieving establish the significance of the deceased and their loss. Adults find it easier to "let go" after the death of a spouse than after the death of a child. The difference centers on the matter of significance. The deceased spouse had a chance to establish identity and significance through their life. A child who dies often does not live long enough to complete this task. The parent is left feeling they must establish significance for the child. One viewpoint of establishing significance of deceased children is to make sure that they are not forgotten. Widows can say good-bye to a mate because significance is there. A parent finds it hard to say good-bye to the child because the significance was not established.

Finding the significance of the deceased is the beginning of reconstruction.

## Signpost of Reorganization

### *Reconstruction begins with acceptance*

When mourners stumble into the Signpost of Reorganization and Reconstruction, they begin to accept the loss and realize that the dark grief clouds are moving. And the Door of Comfort is nearby. They might be a while finding it, but for the first time since entering the Garden Maze they know they will survive the pain and live again. They begin to open up to the future. Somehow life does begin to taste good again.

Manning reminds us that the grieving do not forget the loss nor do they want to. "We are not trying to forget loved ones. We are trying to learn to live with them not being here. We will never forget and should never be asked to do so."[26]

Walsh describes this Signpost this way. "We must wait for the pain to pass into pleasurable memories and for the tears to pass into tenuous acceptance, for life to pass into death, and mourning to pass into laughter and dancing."[27]

At this Signpost the mourner begins to take pleasure in the memories of the deceased. This is unlike the Signpost of Yearning when the memories brought sadness and loneliness.

At the Signpost of Reconstruction we begin to put our loss into a perspective we can deal with. Even as adults we find ourselves somehow like children when a parent dies. Ralph Waldo Emerson wrote, "Sorrow makes us all children again."

In a letter Dr. James Dobson wrote in March 1992, he quotes what his father had written about his grandfather's death.

> At five minutes to four o'clock. . . I remember that I stood at his left side: I smoothed back the hair from his forehead, and laid my hand on his big old red head, so very much like my own. I felt the fever that precedes death: 105. While I was standing there a change came over me. Instead of being a grown man (I was twenty-four at the time) I became a little boy again. They say this often happens to adults who witness the death of a parent. I thought I was in the Union Train Station in Shreveport, Louisiana, in the later afternoon, and I was watching for his return. The old Kansas City Southern passenger train was backing into the station and I saw it come 'round the curve. My heart swelled with pride. I turned to the little boy standing next to me and said, "You see that big man standing on the back of the train, one hand on the air brake and the other on the little whistle with which he signals the engineer? That big man is my dad!" He sat the air brakes and I heard the wheels grind to a stop. I saw him step off that last coach, I ran and jumped into his arms. I gave him a hug and smelled the train smoke on his clothes. "Daddy, I love you," I said.
>
> It all comes back. I patted that big hand and said, "Goodbye, Dad," as he was sinking fast, now. "We haven't forgotten how hard you worked to send five boys and one girl through college: how you wore those old conductor uniforms until they were slick — doing without — that we might have things that we didn't really need. . ."[28]

Two actions that help the mourner with reconstruction is writing and retreating. Retreating does not mean running from reality of the death, but that the mourner often needs to find time and a place to sort out the emotions and memories. When Jesus learned of the beheading of John the Baptist, He sought to have time alone to cope with His loss and journey through the Garden Maze.[29] He chose a mountain top for this retreat. After the death and funeral of my Grandpa Atkins, I spent a morning alone flyfishing for steelhead on my favorite stretch of river. During the funeral I was ministering to the needs of others and now I needed time to cope with the loss myself.

I wrote a story about that morning's fishing — catching and *releasing* a steelhead trout. It was published under the title "Good-Bye." Which brings up another reconstructive action — writing about your loss. This grief writing, as we will see later, can take the form of a personal diary — like C.S. Lewis's *A Grief Observed* — or poetry like the Appalachian tradition of publishing elegies in the local newspapers. These and other reconstructive activities we will discuss in detail in Chapter Seven.

## Tell Me a Story . . .

I do not know why personal stories touch people so deeply and provide such healing, but they do. Stories of the deceased guide us between the Signposts of grief. The funeral service can become a healing catalyst in the mourner's journey through the Garden Maze — more on that healing catalyst in Chapter Six.

When my grandfather died I found that preparing for the funeral helped me stumble through the first steps of healing. Recounting stories of family reunions moved me past the paralysis of shock. Sharing with loved ones at the "viewing times" and seeing his body in the casket, directly confronted my denial. Memories of his teasing all the grandkids guided me as I dealt with sadness and depression. All the funeral activities: the visiting, the stories, the recollections, and the funeral sermon itself confirmed my loss. Before the funeral, I knew intellectually he was gone. After the funeral, emotionally I felt it. The memories were still vivid, there was more healing ahead, but the funeral told me it was time to move on. The funeral helped me accept his death.

My experience was not unique. Consider Lois Duncan's story from "Funerals Are for the Living."

> I went over to the casket and looked down at my mother-in-law. To my surprise, I felt in control of my emotions. I had grown used to the figure in the box — and to the fact that it was only the shell that once had encased a person I loved. I felt a bond with others who had gathered to say good-bye. In three days, we had traveled together through the stages of grief — shock, denial, outrage, bitterness — and had come, at last, to the final one: acceptance.
>
> My husband and I returned home and fell back easily into the normal pattern of our lives. Every time I went to the mailbox, it seemed strangely empty. I kept thinking of things to share with my mother-in-law, particularly news about her grandchildren. I felt frustrated by my inability to send her messages. I did not, however, awake shrieking her name in the night. And although my husband dreamed about his mother often, the dreams were not painful. They were, instead, pleasant interludes of nostalgic reminiscence in which Mom baked his favorite pie or played the piano at a family gathering. He was able to enjoy his memories for what they were — treasured recollections of times that would not recur.[30]

## The Door of Comfort

Once mourners come to full acceptance of their loss and they begin reconstructing their lives they leave the Garden Maze of grief, only to realize that the Maze they were in is life itself. They realize that the Signposts of Grief are outside their own Garden Maze. They stumble into them less often, but times, people, situations, and events will confront them with a Signpost that they had thought they had left in the Garden. Remember the Signposts are *not* stationary.

Almost a year after my father-in-law died, I was confronted by one of the Signposts. Carol and I stopped at a car dealership in our search for a new car. The sales-man we bought from was nicknamed "Tiger." Subconsciously I knew I could deal with Tiger but that I would have to be careful. Later I realized how I knew I could deal with him. His personality was so much like my father-in-law. Tiger was about the same age as my father-in-law, he had the same German build, same facial expressions, and his pants drooped and his shirt-tail hung out. We liked Tiger. We bought the car. But a normally joyful occasion was a time of renewed grief for us. Tiger reminded us how much we missed dickering and dealing with Dad. I found myself far outside of the Garden Maze and yet staring at the Signpost of Yearning.

When our friends wander between the Signposts of grief, they stumble among yearning, depression, despair, denial, and acceptance. We cannot point their way; they must find their own way. What can we do to comfort them?

Sometimes, as we will see next, all they need is *our ears*.

# Chapter 3

# Don't Talk... Listen

## When to Say Nothing
## What Not to Say

*He who has ears to hear*
*Let them hear.*[31]
—Jesus

*There is an appointed time for everything.*
*A time to weep, and a time to laugh;*
*A time to mourn, and a time to dance.*
*A time to embrace, and a time to shun embracing.*
*A time to be silent, and a time to speak.*[32]
—The Preacher

When we do find the courage to visit the mourning we tend to fill every silent moment with speech. Somehow we are uncomfortable with silence, and even more uncomfortable with listening. In part because, as we noted earlier, that we think we must have an answer for every question that the grieving pose. Or that we should defend God when they vent their anger towards Him. Or that we must "be ready to give an answer for the hope that dwells within us."

But in fact we have no answer to many of the questions the mourning pose. Fortunately many of the questions and most of the anger at God are the mind and emotions struggling to cope with the pain of the loss. What they need during those times is not theological or philosophical answers but rather to be heard. Having someone to talk to who will listen as a sounding board without being critical, without trying to have all the answers, will allow the grieving to express their emotions. And once they are in the open and they hear themselves, then healing and acceptance can begin. We just have to be present and willing to listen.

*Remember, the goal of the mourning is not to forget the deceased or the loss.* They want instead to know if they will survive the pain and learn to cope with their loss. Sometimes the most comforting action we can perform is to go with them until they can find a silent place to speak their heart's cry. Albert Walsh in his book *Reflections of Death and Grief,* wrote about a man whose wife (Janet)

was terminally ill. Walsh wrote of the restlessness of this home where silence is avoided at all costs. "Can death be kept away if we don't think about it?" If someone wasn't chattering, the television blared to keep out the silence.
Walsh wrote:

> I had only one opportunity to be with Janet's husband (Harry) alone. He had invited me to go rabbit hunting with him...
>
> From the moment I arrived that day, Harry talked. He talked first about his gun, then necessary preparations for the hunt, then the place and the abundance of game, on and on and on. Harry talked and talked, with the exception of one moment I will remember for the rest of my life.
>
> We had covered most of the trail Harry always hunted without seeing any game. Feeling somewhat exhausted we sat together on the trunk of a fallen tree and looked out over the valley below. There were minutes of silence with only the occasional cawing of a crow in the distance. I felt my muscles relax for the first time all day. Harry, on the other hand, seemed agitated, restless, at first twisting his gunstock in the dry leaves making a sharp crackling sound, then peeling away at the dead bark on the tree trunk.
>
> Finally Harry rested his weary soul as well. It was as though his spirit found an inner place of solitude. This became evident to me when first I noticed a certain, almost unexplainable, stillness between us and around us. He was the first to break the stillness with these words: "Bert, I don't know what I'll do without Janet. I don't need her, I mean, I can certainly survive without her. I love her and I really don't know what life will be like when she's gone. How do I raise the kids? I know she's dying, I know I'm losing her." Harry's spirit was still, and in this experience he had discovered the courage and ability to speak of what would be.
>
> Following his words I asked, "Harry, how do you feel now, at this moment?" He answered, "O.K. I guess," then quickly added, "No! I'm not O.K., I hurt inside. At times I'm so confused and tormented. But just now I feel like I can accept whatever will be. I felt a peace, like the voices shut up for awhile, you know?" A stilling of anxious thoughts and voices gave opportunity for acceptance and then peace.[33]

Walsh's experience illustrates one of the most powerful concepts in grief ministry — the power of the ear.

More than they need to hear, they need to *be heard*.

More than we need to speak, we need to *listen*.

## The Ministry of *Presence*

In the Greek language of the New Testament the word translated as "comfort" is also translated in many texts as "encouragement," and in one as "advocate" — I John 2:1. It was also the Greek equivalent for Barnabas' name — "Son of Encouragement." He could also be called "Son of Comfort." The Greek word for comfort and encouragement literally means, "called to stand alongside." That is the comfort that Barnabas brought to an outcast named Saul, who returned to Jerusalem a Christian but no one would "stand alongside" him. No one, that is, except Barnabas. As a result this Saul became the great missionary, the Apostle Paul. Later Barnabas "stood alongside" a young man John Mark, who had failed them on the first missionary journey. But through the *comfort* of Barnabas he became the author of the Gospel of Mark.

In John 14:16-18, Jesus called Himself a "Comforter." He stated that once He leaves the disciples, they will not be left alone like "orphans" but they will have another "Comforter," the Holy Spirit, to guide them.

Comfort and encouragement both have aspects of communication but their greatest quality is *presence*.

When we grieve we need a *Barnabas* to stand beside us. Like the little girl who was afraid at bedtime said, "Mommy, will you stay with me? I know God is here, but I need someone with skin on."

Walsh touches on the power of presence,

So often we struggle for some word of comfort when what

the bereaved really needs and desires is to be embraced, or
simply touched, to share tears that reflect a profound sense of
loss on the part of the minister as well as the one being ministered to.[34]

# The Power of Listening

For the grieving, the encouraging and supportive
friends are those who "lay ears" on them. They listen
instead of seeking to fix the situation. They empathize
with them, not try to *explain* to them. They stay with
them without trying to put a better face on it. These listening friends are the encouragers.

### The Encourager

If I really cared
Who you are would be more important to me than who
I am.
Where you hurt would be more important than that I'm
well.
What you feel would be more important than what I
know.
I'd look you in the eyes when you talk to me;
I'd think about what you are saying rather than what I'm
going to say next.
I'd hear your feelings as well as your words.
I'd listen without defending.
I'd hear without deciding whether you are right or
wrong.
I'd ask you why and how, not just when and where.
I'd allow you inside me
I'd tell you my hopes, my dreams, my fears, my hurts;
I'd tell you when I've blown it and when I've made it.
I'd laugh with you, and not at you
I'd talk with you, and not to you, and
I'd know when it's time to do neither.
I wouldn't climb your walls
I'd wait until you let me in the gate.

I wouldn't unlock your secrets
  I'd wait until you handed me the key.
I'd leave my solutions at home and put away my scripts;
  the performances would end.
If I really cared about you
  I'd be myself with you
And give you the right
  to be the same.

—Author Unknown

## Listening to the Mourning and Dying

"I am worn out for groaning; all night long I flood my bed with weeping and drench my couch with tears."[35]

The grieving and dying have a lot of disquieting things to say. It is not easy to hear a loved one request to die, or speak of their own death. After a long struggle with pain and illness the dying often long for rest that death will bring. But we do not want to let them go, for their rest begins our loss. It is not easy to listen.

> I was not comfortable with their pain and their tears. I would do anything to keep from having to deal with people in grief. I thought my job was to cheer everyone up. I would tell jokes at inappropriate times. I would quote scripture. I am sure there are people who would love to cram the King James version down my throat to this day. I thought if I got a family through the funeral without tears, I had done a great job of comforting. I was taking their grief away from them.[36]

The dying want to find one person that they can talk to about their fears and misgivings and who will listen to their concerns for family they leave behind, and to listen to their fears about death itself. Sometimes they choose a friend to speak to about their passage. Other times they choose a complete stranger, like a nurses' aide or a housekeeper at a hospital — at night when the terminally ill become restless the healthcare staff often become their sounding boards. These servants provide an important ministry. "The greatest of you shall be the servant of all."

*Listening is a servant's chore, but before we can listen we must be silent.*

Walsh wrote,

> I believe we must think first of the time in which we should be silent. This should never be a purposeless silence, a silence which merely disguises our inability to say anything at all, an inability which stems from our own insecurities and uncertainties. Rather, we should carefully choose to be silent . . . to make ourselves available for hearing what the bereaved and dying have to share.
>
> The dying and the bereaved will write on the pages of our lives their own words and phrases, inscribed with the painful ink of their heart's pen. They will tell us their most penetrating concerns and misgivings. If we can remain silent long enough, soon we will receive the vital telegram of the mind's messenger of those who hurt so deeply.[37]

## Jesus Spoke of His Death

When Jesus knew His death was quickly approaching, He felt overwhelmed with feelings and wanted to talk to His closest disciples about it. And He wanted them to care and understand. I wonder if before His death they did. The garden scene indicates that they did not.

"My soul is overwhelmed with sorrow to the point of death. Stay here and keep watch with me . . . . My Father, if it is possible, may this cup be taken from me. Yet not as I will, but as you will."[38]

In the garden Jesus confirms His humanity through His genuine anxieties and fears — He was Mary's Son. He also demonstrated His divinity through His resolve to do "not My will but Yours" — He was God's Son. The fears and anxieties Jesus expressed reflect our own, embrace our own, embody our own.

I have too often responded to the grieving like the disciples did — at rest while the mourner is restless. All He requested was their *presence* and alertness. "Stay here and keep watch." Jesus spoke to God and felt God's closeness. Even the angels attended to His needs but wanted His friends to be close and to care. They slept. Too often I have too, while the dying lay restless.

"Death is more often than not an experience in isolation, one which brings us to the brink of loneliness and despair. . . we do not want to be alone."[39]

Manning writes of "a dying ritual" as the chance for the dying to talk and be heard. Being heard is what all people need, but it may be the hardest for them to find.

> We let people die in loneliness and fear because our own fear of death will not let us face the ultimate intimacy and give people dying rituals.
>
> There was a time when we allowed people to have the rituals of dying. My grandfather died while still a young man. Something poisonous bit him, and since modern medicines were not available, he died in a period of a few days. No one tried to tell him he was not going to die. He had a special time with each of his children. He called them one by one to his side, and they talked about his dying. That allowed him the rituals of dying. Dying rituals allow people the chance to work through their feeling and prepare for the passage. . .
>
> The issue is not whether they should know [that they are dying]. The issue is do we dare face it with them.[40]

Listening is the beauty and ministry of *Hospice*. Someone has said that Christ's time on the mount of transfiguration, when Moses and Elijah visited with Him before his death in Jerusalem, was the first "hospice visit." The last month of His life Jesus spoke often to His Apostles about His approaching death. Following the Mount of Transfiguration Jesus opened His heart again to speak with these three disciples about His death. But Peter did not want to speak of Jesus' death and tried to find a way to alleviate the fear of losing his dear friend, Jesus. Peter was in denial of Jesus' approaching death. "Cannot we build tabernacles and celebrate the Passover here and avoid Jerusalem and this topic all together?" Peter seemed to ask.[41]

Jesus became angry at Peter's avoidance tactics and I wonder what else He may have shared with them if they would have only been silent enough to listen. We do not know what He might have said then but we do know what tore at His heart from the cross. The statements of Jesus on the cross — like the statements of dying people — express what is dearest to Him. His followers remembered clearly what Jesus said from the cross, like a family hovering over the bed of a dying family member. They repeat every word the dying says. They ask others to be quiet. They hang on every word. They knew that you do not have the privilege of asking a dying person to repeat what he says, because every breath may be his last.

From the cross Jesus spoke about family and His concern for those dependent upon Him. He said, "John, take care of My mother."[42] Given a chance, would He have asked that of John while they were on the mount of transfiguration?

In "I thirst"[43] Jesus depicts the pain of the dying and embodies our own pain. The dying often express their pain even when they know you can do nothing to ease it. It is enough that you are there to hear and care.

Christ mentions His desire to heal broken relationships when He said, "Father forgive them for they do not know what they do."[44] The dying frequently express misgivings about relationships gone astray. No one's fences are completely mended.

Jesus comforted others in His hour of death when He spoke of the future and of Paradise. He promised the dying thief, "Today, you will be with Me in Paradise."[45]

Christians on their deathbeds often minister to their visitors as much as they are ministered to — their statements of faith encourage us.

Jesus expressed His feelings about the closeness of God, "My God, My God, Why have You forsaken Me?"[46] This statement is usually taken to mean that Jesus felt alone on the cross, but I think we stop short by saying that this is only what the statement means. The statement in the Hebrew language, *Eloi, Eloi, lama sabachthani,*[47] was a quote from Psalm 22:1. It was the first line of a hymn that the followers — and Jesus — sang since childhood in the local synagogue. When Jesus quoted that line, He not only expressed His feeling that God *seemed* distant but that he was meditating on that Psalm — that childhood song. Even a quick reading of Psalm 22 shows that the writer David went from the loneliness of the first lines to the assurance of God's love and nearness in verse 24, "For He [God] has not despised or disdained the suffering of the afflicted one; He has not hidden His face from him but has listened to his cry for help."

If on my deathbed my family hears me crying, "I was sinking deep in sin far from the peaceful shore; very deeply stained within sinking to rise no more . . ." they will not feel despair about my plight or salvation. They know *the rest of the song.* "But the Master of the sea heard my despairing cry, and from the waters lifted me now safe am I! Love lifted me, Love lifted me. . . ."

I wonder if we miss all of what Jesus declared when He quoted the first line of Psalm 22. Did that Psalm mean to Jesus what "Love Lifted Me" means to me? After all Psalm 22:16, 18 say, "A band of evil men has encircled me, they have pierced my hands and feet. . . . They divide my garments among them and cast lots for my clothing." I think Christ's quotation declared more than His sense of loneliness. It proclaimed His faith in God, who would turn this evil into good! In one breath He stated His feeling of loneliness and His vision of victory. He stated, "This seems lonely now but I know God will bring the victory." Such is often the sentiment of a Christian before their death.

On the cross Jesus also showed His acceptance of death with His words, "Father, into Your hands I commit my spirit."[48] People of faith who know they are about to die will often share with family and friends their acceptance of the situation. At times they also need permission to die, Jesus gave Himself that permission when He said, "It is finished."[49]

My writing friend, Delores Bius, wrote a story called, "Coping With The Big 'C'," a story of Jay, a teenager trying to deal with his dad's struggle and death to cancer. Jay and his dad were very close but Jay could not bring himself to go the hospital. Herein we see the need for survivors to hear the words of the dying; also it shows how a concerned friend *listened* then helped.

> In the hospital, Fred McGowan had gotten well acquainted with one of the volunteers who shaved some of the men and got them newspapers. . . Bob Michaels, a former cardiac patient who began doing volunteer work as a therapy, was a Christian and considered the hospital a mission field. As brothers in Christ, the two men had a lot in common. Fred talked much with Bob about this cancer and the process of dying.
>
> One day Fred admitted to Bob, "I know I'm dying, and in a way it's a relief. As Paul put it, 'we are confident, I say, and willing rather to be absent from the body, and to be present with the Lord' [II Corinthians 5:8]. I know that my long sleep will seem like nothing, and the next thing I'll see is Christ returning." A smile brightened his eyes. "You know, it's strange, but seeing Christ is more real to me now than this hospital or my old beat-up body."
>
> He reached for the button that would raise the head of his

bed. Bob stepped up and adjusted his pillow. After a sip of water, Mr. McGowan continued. "My wife and I have discussed my dying, and she can accept it, but my son is really having a tough time coping. If he could only comprehend that cancer can happen to anyone — even a Christian — and that I'll receive a new body at the resurrection, he might find it easier to accept my death."

"Maybe I could help," Bob suggested. As a member of the Supportive Care Team on the cancer floor, he often helped patients and their loved ones work through to acceptance of death.

That night Bob Michaels phoned Jay, introduced himself, and asked if Jay would have dinner with him the following day after school. At first Jay was a little wary, but he finally agreed.

The next day, over hearty soup, thick crusty bread, and salad at a nearby restaurant, Bob told Jay that he too was a Christian. "You see, Jay, I took the loss of my perfect health pretty hard at first. I had been active all my life, working out with weights, playing racquetball, and such. After my heart attack, at only 28, I felt like an invalid. But then I began to realize this body is nothing in comparison with the perfect one the Lord is going to give me one day."

"However, Jay," he continued, "I realize that it is pretty rough for a young fellow like you to cope with seeing your father so disfigured by illness. I know you'd rather remember your dad as he used to be, not as he is now. But if you stay away from him now, you'll have guilt feelings to struggle with after he dies. You need him now as much as he needs you. Then, afterward, you'll still remember how he looked when he was well. And you'll know that the next time you see him he'll be in perfect health." The man's smile softened his words. He reached out and touched Jay's arm.

"Jay, I'd urge you to visit your dad before it's too late. I know it's hard, but once you take the first few steps into his room, the worst is over."

Later that night when Fred McGowan was lying in bed unable to sleep, he suddenly felt someone take his hand. He looked up and found his son standing there. Tears rolled down his cheeks, Jay looked at his father.

"It's all right, son. I'll have a new body someday. A perfect one!"

Squeezing his hand, Jay assured him, "I know, Dad. It was hard at first for me to accept your not getting well. I kept thinking we'd conquer the big 'C.' But then I had a long talk with Bob. He pointed out to me that only your body has changed, not the real you. I can handle your not getting well now, Dad, if you can!"

Tears welled up in Dad's eyes and trickled down his cheeks. "I'm getting anxious to escape this pain, Jay. And I am looking forward to meeting Jesus. He's become very close to me these past few weeks. For me. . . it will seem just a moment until His return. He squeezed Jay's hand. "But it's a relief to know we can say our goodbyes and be together at the end just as we'll be together again in heaven."

Jay pulled up a chair and sat down close to the bed. Mom waited outside, but she wouldn't mind. He knew there'd be some rough days still ahead, but knowing the Lord was with him, he could manage.[50]

# Caring for Caregivers

The caregivers who stand daily by the side of a dying loved one need our support and listening ear too. They often feel overwhelmed with the burden of caring for the dying friend or relative. They have to cope with their own feelings of loss and sometimes guilt — for wishing it was over — as Doug Manning writes about caring for his dying father.

My father decided to die on July 5, 1985. It took him eight months to complete his mission. During those months I tried to arrange my schedule to be with him and care for needs. That was tough because I make my living speaking all over the country.

No one told me how tiring that can become. No one told me how it feels to get home past midnight dead tired, only to need to go to one's father's side for another time of crisis. No one told me how to react when I put him in the bathtub, and he promptly messed in the water. No one told me that I would want to pull the stopper on the tub and let him go down the drain.

60

No one told me that I would want it to be over. That means I was ready for my father to die. I wanted it to be over because he was in a race with pain, and I wanted him to win. I also wanted it to be over because I was tired and needed some relief. These feelings are normal.[51]

## Careful, Do Not Say This . . .

I am afraid to write the next paragraph because it is difficult enough for most people to visit a mourning or dying friend, but there are some things that are better left unsaid. Perhaps knowing them, you will become more comfortable about what you do say because you will know some of the things you should not say.

Most of the comfort grieving people receive comes from friends. Unfortunately most of the hurt they endure is also from their friends. The following statements, among others like them, sound good on the surface but you do not have to listen long to grieving people to realize that they often hurt.

Comfort, as we have suggested before, comes when the mourning learn that we see the significance of their loss and of their dead loved one. The following comments are efforts at comforting, but they end up trivializing the mourners' feelings. Trivializing angers grieving people.

Part of the problem with many statements is not that they are wrong or hurtful in themselves but that they appear trite to grieving — who admittedly are illogical at times. C.S. Lewis offers some insight into a mixture of losses that survivors experience when grieving. When for instance a mother loses a daughter, the mother mourns the loss (sometimes separately) of several aspects. She loses a daughter, a friend, her future activities with her daughter, and even her daughter's future — what she had dreamed for her daughter and what she knew of her

A COMFORTING WORD

daughter's dreams. At times mourners can let go of different aspects of the deceased, while they still mourn others. Comments can be comforting or trite depending on which loss the mourner is lamenting when that statement is made. That is another reason why *listening* is so important.

> And poor C. [his friend] quotes to me, "Do not mourn like those that have no hope." It astonishes me, the way we are invited to apply to ourselves words so obviously addressed to our betters. What St. Paul says can comfort only those who love God better than the dead, and the dead better than themselves. If a mother is mourning not for what she has lost but for what her dead child has lost, it is a comfort to believe that the child has not lost the end for which it was created. And it is a comfort to believe that she herself, in losing her chief or only natural happiness, has not lost a greater thing, that she may still hope to "glorify God and enjoy Him forever." A comfort to the God-aimed, eternal spirit within her. But not to her motherhood. The specifically maternal happiness must be written off. Never, in any place or time, will she have her son on her knees, or bathe him, or tell him a story, or plan for his future, or see her grandchild.[52]

Here are some untimely remarks that appear trite to the mourning.

"*God must have wanted her more than you do. . . .*" The grieving respond, "God has so many people in heaven, why did He want one more? He couldn't want her more than I want and need her here. What will I do without her?"

"*They're in a better place. . . .*" Parents of the children think, "Then God thinks I couldn't take care of them."

"*He is not hurting any more. . . .*" His widow responds, "Maybe that's true, but I'm hurting. How can a loving, all-powerful God do this to me or allow this to happen? How can I live on without him?"

"*I understand how you feel . . . though he wasn't a child,*

62

*my dog, Simbad was very special to me. . . ."* Saying that we *understand* another's grief is very unsteady ground unless you have experienced a loss as significant as the loss of the one you seek to comfort. Talking about a dead dog will not suffice. This is not to say that the loss of a pet is not a loss that people do not or should not mourn. But that loss will not comfort nor compare with the loss of a child, spouse, or friend.

*"You can just try again and have another baby . . . ."* and *"That child must have not been right for you so God will send a better one. . . ."* are frequent comments after a couple experiences a miscarriage. But this comment treats the loss as insignificant. To the couple it is traumatic.

*"Your child died, but it could have been worse; it could have been two children – so cheer up."* This comment trivializes the loss of the child and the couple's loss. People who dismiss the loss or somehow imply that it was a blessing leave the impression that the person did not matter.

When a person is facing certain death people sometimes tell the dying person and their family, *"A miracle can always happen,"* or *"We never know what tomorrow will hold."* Better is a simple acknowledgement of love and compassion.

Sometimes we are not straightforward with children about the death of a loved one. We couch the death in such soft terms that the children often wonder what happened. We softly say that, *"Jesus took the person because He loved him,"* then expect the child to sing "Jesus Loves Me" in Bible School. We say, *"The person went to sleep,"* and then wonder why the child is afraid to go to bed.

When the dying are angry at God, wish they were dead, or they want to die, we say *"Oh! Come on now, I know you really don't mean that; you really don't feel that way!"*

The dying have no time or energy for word games and saying things they do not mean; we will do the dying a grave injustice with such negation of their true feelings. It would be far better for us to be honest and say something like, "I find what you are saying hard to accept, it hurts to hear you talk this way."[53]

When we say, *"God will not put more on us than we can bear,"* we are saying, *"This loss is not an unbearable burden."* We trivialize the loss.

At a widow's first Christmas alone someone said, *"I know you must be hurting this Christmas season, but isn't it a great comfort knowing that Carl is spending his first Christmas with the Lord."*

She replied, "No, it is no comfort at all. He should be spending it with me."[54]

Delores Bius described a better approach when she wrote,

A few weeks ago, I noticed a lady in our congregation looking especially sad during worship services. Her husband had died a few months earlier. After the postlude, I said: "Marie, how are you doing? I saw by the calendar that Les's birthday is next week, and I know it must be hard for you. I wanted you to know I'll be thinking of you and praying for you. Les was such an active part of our Sunday School class, and it just isn't the same without him."

Rather than being depressed by my reminder of his husband, Marie's face shone at my understanding of her feelings. "Yes, I'll especially miss Les on his birthday as it is Father's Day too, and Les was always recognized as the oldest father in the congregation on that day. It will be hard, but I am grateful for your prayers and thoughtfulness," she remarked.[55]

## Acknowledging Their Loss

Manning suggests that acknowledging the loss is the best way to approach the griever. This recognizes the loss instead of trivializing it.

It seems to be the opposite of what will help people but we need to understand and relate to the loss as a loss. "Your husband died, and I know you must be devastated. A huge chunk has been bitten out of your heart, and it will not grow back. You will learn to live again, but the chunk will never grow back."[56]

While struggling through grief many people ask, "How can a good, all-powerful God allow suffering?"

The answer to that question comes next.

# Chapter 4

# Death and the "Will of God"

## Why People Suffer

*Not that I am (I think) in much danger of ceasing to believe in God.*
*The real danger is of coming to believe such dreadful things about Him.*
*The conclusion I dread is not, "So there's no God after all," but,*
*"So this is what God's really like. Deceive yourself no longer."*[57]
—C.S. Lewis

In a time of intense grief C.S. Lewis questioned the goodness of God. His questioning is not uncommon among mourners.

One afternoon after our teenaged paperboy, Darrold "Skeeter" Winters, delivered the papers in our neighborhood, he dashed across an intersection on his bike and was struck by a truck. It was an unfortunate — and fatal — accident.

Skeeter's mom, dad, and sister were shocked and grief-stricken.

Because the Winters family had no church home, they had the Funeral Director, Louis Juday, ask me to speak at Skeeter's funeral. After we had agreed on the date and time Louis hesitated.

"One more thing, Kenn," Louis said. "The mother insists that her son wear a T-shirt in the casket. I tried to convince her otherwise but she insisted."

"Is it a special T-shirt?" I asked.

"Apparently, it was one of Skeeter's favorite shirts," Louis answered. "It has a picture of a donkey on a podium with its rear-end to the front. And it reads, 'When I die they will bury me faced down so you can kiss my _____.'"

"Oh, I see . . ." I said.

"Kenn," Louis asked, "What can we do?"

"Will it be a closed casket service?"

"They want it open," Louis answered.

"Why put such a defiant shirt on him?" I asked. "I wonder if she is angry with God for 'taking her son.'"

"I think someone told her that Skeeter's death was 'the will of God' and that she should accept it because of that," Louis said.

That afternoon my visit with the Winters family confirmed that Skeeter's mom was bitter and angry with God for "taking her son from her."

Some well-meaning person had told her, "We don't understand it but it must fit into God's will. Skeeter's time was up. And God must have wanted him more than you do, so He took him."

Skeeter's mom questioned the character of a God who would snatch her teenaged son from her in such a violent way.

She wondered, "How could God be good and all-powerful and cause such suffering?"

Good question.

As C.S. Lewis found out, the reality of this question hits us only when we are struck by tragedy.

> Bridge-players tell me that there must be some money on the game, "or else people won't take it seriously." Apparently it's like that. Your bid — for God or no God, for a good God or the Cosmic Sadist, for eternal life or nonentity — will not be serious if nothing much is staked on it. And you will never discover how serious it was until the stakes are raised horribly high; until you find that you are playing not for counters or for sixpences but for every penny you have in the world. Nothing less will shake a man — or at any rate a man like me — out of his merely verbal thinking and his merely notional beliefs. He has to be knocked silly before he comes to his senses. Only torture will bring out the truth. Only under torture does he discover it himself.[58]

In this chapter we will discuss the illogical assumption that God has preset the death date for everyone. We'll consider God's providence, our personal freedom and suffering, especially as it relates to death, comforting the survivors, and leading them beyond the bitterness that this misinformation causes.

# The Confusion About Death and God's Will

It surprises me how deep the confusion about the issue of death and the will of God runs among both the churched and unchurched. People utter statements like, "When your number is up; it's up!" "When God is ready for you, He'll call you home." The thought is that everyone has a personal clock counting down the time before he will exit this world.

This widespread presumption is expressed by songs like "Last Kiss," sung by Jay Frank Wilson. The song says that the girlfriend died in a car accident when they swerved to miss a stalled car on a rainy night.

Here's the chorus of this popular hit from 1961:

"Where oh, where can my baby be?
The Lord took her away from me,
She's gone to heaven so I've got to be good,
So I can see my Baby, when I leave this world."

This number one song hit a double in theological bloopers. The worst error is that heaven can be earned by good works, "I've got to *be good* so I can see my baby when I leave this world." Trusting our works leads to death; trusting God's grace, Jesus' merit and His cleansing blood leads to life.

The song's second blunder teaches that "the Lord *took her* away . . . ." If that statement is true it raises several questions. If it was God's will, did He *create* the accident to "take her"? Did He cause the other car to stall on the curve that rainy night? Or, do we deem it God's will because He did not stop the accident? Or, do we cry "God's will" because He did not miraculously rescue her from the fatal injuries?

How much of our lives does God program and control? Is He a puppeteer who pulls the strings and jerks us off stage? I question the assumption that no person leaves this world unless it's God's specific will and in His timing, place, and manner.

What about the people who step out of God's will and use their freedom to defy God, such as those who commit suicide? Are they simply acting as agents of God's will? Certainly not.

How about murder victims? Are their deaths a part of God's will when murder specifically defies many commands of Scripture?

How about accidental deaths like Skeeter's? If an accident was the will of God — that is His *intention* — then it is a designed event and is no longer an accident.

What about death by illness? Is our mismanagement of our health simply a predetermined Divine plan? What about the people who overeat, neglect their high blood pressure, and die young from a heart attack? Is their death God's will or a result of their neglect of natural laws?

How can so many contradictory statements be sheltered equally under the umbrella of "God's will?"

Accepted blindly, the popular view that death is the predetermined will of God, leads us to confusion and bitterness rather than comfort.

If each specific death is the will of God, are we acting in rebellion against God if we save someone from death's clutches?

After a man's wife died the husband said to his minister, Bob Palmer, "Well, I must just accept it. It's the will of God."

But as a doctor, he had been fighting for her life. He had called in the best specialists. He had used all the devices of modern science to fight disease. Was he fighting the will of God all that time? If she had recovered, would he have called her recovery, the will of God? We cannot have it both ways. The woman's recovery and the woman's death cannot equally be the will of God in the sense of being His *intention*.

A mother weeping in anguish over the death of her baby said, "I suppose it's the will of God, but if only the doctor had come in time, he could have saved my baby." If the doctor had come in time, would he have been able to outwit the will of God?

Remember what the Scriptures said of Job after he suffered so much, including the death of all his children? "In all this Job did not sin, nor blame God" (Job 1:21 [NASB]). If God had "taken Job's children" the blame would squarely rest on God's shoulders.

## God's Will and Our Freedom

Where does the providential will of God and the free choice of mankind meet when it comes to suffering and death?

Our good and omnipotent God granted us freedom in moral choices and natural choices — that is to employ natural objects. This freedom resulted in the abuse of the choices which brought suffering into the world. People suffer because of wrong moral choices, from abuse or neglect of natural laws, or because their lives are intertwined with millions of others who are abusing or neglecting moral and natural laws. To stop this suffering God would have to withhold freedom, because freedom implies the ability to choose between two alternatives — obedience and disobedience.

The following discussion is an overview of this theme as it applies to death, mourning, and funerals. For a complete discussion of suffering read *A Loving God In A Suffering World*, by Jon Tal Murphree.[59]

## Three Reasons People Suffer

The reasons people suffer — and ultimately die — fit

into three categories. People suffer because of unrighteousness; the abuse of God's moral laws. People suffer because of righteousness sake; the keeping of God's moral codes. People suffer because we live in a "dangerous world" where people affect one another through their abuse and neglect of moral or natural laws.

## Suffering Because of *Unrighteousness*

"For what credit is there if you sin and are harshly treated, you endure it with patience?" (1 Peter 2:20 [NASB]).

Peter declares that Christian slaves gain no merit when they patiently endure harsh treatment from their masters after they rebel against God's moral law (such as stealing from their master). Peter directly connects their "harsh treatment" with their "sin" — their transgression of God's moral code.

"By no means let any of you suffer as a murderer, or thief, or evildoer, or a troublesome meddler;" (1 Peter 4:15 [NASB]).

Here Peter again connects suffering with disobedience to God's moral law. He mentions the suffering of murders, thieves, evildoers, and meddlers without sighting an agent of wrath.

> For rulers hold no terror for those who do right, but for those who do wrong. Do you want to be free from fear of the one in authority? Then do what is right and he will commend you. For he is God's servant to do you good. But if you do wrong, be afraid, for he does not bear the sword for nothing. He is God's servant, an agent of wrath to bring punishment on the wrongdoer (Romans 13:3-4).

Paul refers to government as an agent of wrath, who brings punishment on wrongdoers even unto death. The Roman government used swords for capital punishment, not for spankings.

In *A Loving God In A Suffering World*, Jon Tal Murphree says,

> Rather than saying that suffering is penalty for sin, it would be more accurate to say that suffering at times is the effect, the consequence, the automatic fallout of sin. The 'punishment' is included in the scheme of things rather than being imposed directly on individuals.[60]

When God granted Adam and Eve the freedom to choose, He granted them the ability to choose between obedience and disobedience — to eat or not to eat from the tree of the knowledge of good and evil. If He had given them freedom to choose but only one option, they would have had no freedom.

God's dilemma (speaking in human terms) was to grant freedom and risk its abuses, or to withhold freedom, preventing its abuses and the suffering it creates. There is no such thing as freedom without the ability to abuse freedom. Without it, freedom is *not* freedom at all.

Murphree says,

> Without our freedom there might have been no suffering as we know it, but neither could there have been sympathy. There would have been no hatred, but for the same reason there could have been no voluntary love. There would have been no sorrow, but neither could there have been comfort. There would have been no danger, but neither could there have been courage or heroism . . . . Without moral freedom there would be no vice, but by the same token there could have been no virtue; virtue that is not freely chosen is no more than the "virtue" of fire to burn, water to freeze or light to shine. Mechanical robots programmed for certain behavior and deprived of freedom would have no privilege of fellowship with God. Both the very worst in life and the very best are made possible by moral freedom. Freedom itself precludes having the good without the possibility of the bad.[61]

Natural laws are neutral and can be manipulated equally well for evil or for good. We must have natural freedom to facilitate our moral freedom. For example, the laws of spontaneous combustion are used equally well by both the families keeping their homes warm and cooking their food, and the arsonist who destroys businesses and homes.

Moral freedom necessitates natural freedom to move and employ material objects. If we make a moral choice to help the hungry, but cannot manipulate the natural objects, we have no freedom. But the same is true if we make the other moral choice.

Some say that God could stop suffering by programming nature (or individuals) never to do evil. For instance, God could program automobiles to do good (taking children to school, shopping or the hospital) but not to do evil (robbing banks, kidnapping, or allowing drunk driving). But allowing freedom means risking the abuse of that freedom. That abuse — sin — is not desired by God, nor is it His will.

In Jesus' story of the Prodigal Son, the father gave the youngest son his share of the inheritance, so that he had the *freedom to choose*. The father — who models God in the story — gave his son the freedom (that the money created) and risked the son's abuse of that freedom.

A measure of evil and suffering exists because millions, even billions, of free people are choosing daily to use or abuse their moral freedom.

## Suffering for Righteousness' Sake

"But if you do what is right and suffer and patiently endure it, this finds favor with God" (1 Peter 2:20 [NASB]).

Blessed are those who are persecuted because of righteousness, for theirs is the kingdom of Heaven. Blessed are you when people insult you, persecute you and falsely say all kinds of evil against you because of Me. Rejoice and be glad, because great is your reward in Heaven, for in the same way they persecuted the prophets who were before you (Matthew 5:10-12 [NIV]).

"However, if you suffer as a Christian, do not be ashamed, but praise God that you bear that name." (1 Peter 4:16 [NIV]).

These three passages proclaim that people can suffer because of their good deeds. Jesus is the example.

Wasn't Jesus put to death for His good deeds? See 1 Peter 2:18-25. Someone may ask, "Was not the death of Jesus the will of God?"

Yes it was. But consider the uniqueness of that situation. Jesus asked in the garden for the "cup of suffering" — His death — to pass from Him. But, He said, "Not My will, but Yours be done." Death is a result of man's sin. Death was not God's intention, but He sent His Son to destroy the enemy called death, according to 1 Corinthians 15:26. To destroy death Jesus had to die and be raised victoriously over the grave. As Romans 8:28 says, God can turn "all things" including evil and suffering into "good." Jesus' death became our life, forgiveness, and grace.

As a second example of suffering for goodness sake, consider Stephen who was stoned to death for proclaiming his faith in Jesus as the Messiah.[62]

The author of Hebrews mentioned that "by faith . . . some escaped the edge of the sword" while others by that *same faith* "were slain by the sword."[63]

Haralan Popov's book, *Tortured For His Faith*, describes the persecution of Christians under Bulgaria's former communist government. Sergei Kordakov's book, *The Persecutor*, shows his persecution of believers in the former U.S.S.R. and his conversion because of the faithfulness of the suffering Christians he had beaten.

In part Christians suffer because they make correct moral choices and receive the backlash of the world's hatred for the truth.

## Suffering Because We Live in a "Dangerous World"

This category of suffering is the most difficult one to cope with emotionally, because it involves the suffering of innocent victims — victims of the evil actions of others. Victims of accidents because someone abused or neglected natural laws. Victims because our "dangerous world" is filled with disease and natural catastrophes; such as tornadoes, floods, lightning, and hurricanes. Jesus spoke of the death of *innocent* people because of evil actions of others and because of accidents.

> Now there were some present at that time who told Jesus about Galileans whose blood Pilate had mixed with their sacrifices. Jesus answered, "Do you think that these Galileans were worse sinners than all the other Galileans because they suffered this way? I tell you, no! But unless you repent, you too will all perish. Of those eighteen who died when the tower in Siloam fell on them — do you think they were more guilty than all the others who were living in Jerusalem? I tell you, no! But unless you repent, you too will all perish" (Luke 13:1-5).

Not all suffering is connected with a person's response to God's moral laws. Was the death of those Galileans God's will? No. In this case some Galileans suffered because of the immoral actions of an unjust leader who abused his moral freedom and his governmental power.

The sins of one person can often affect innocent people around them; for extreme cases consider rape, incest, and murder.

How can someone's death be God's will when the person who inflicted the fatal blow disobeys God's law in the process? A three-year-old girl rode her tiny tricycle in her front lawn one summer evening after dinner. A drunk driver screamed around the corner, lost control of his vehicle, raced through the yard, then hit and killed the young girl. Trying to comfort the mother someone said, "It was God's will."

But how can it be God's will when no part of the equation was God's will? Was it God's will for the man to be drunk? Was it God's will for him to disobey the civil law about driving while intoxicated? Was it God's will for him to break the speed limit? Was it God's will for him to leave the safe traffic area, cross the lawn and hit a child riding her tricycle? "No" to all of the above.

If the portions of the equation are not God's will then how can the sum total of the given parts become the will of God?

It cannot.

## Death by Accidents

At times, people suffer because *others* have neglected natural laws. Eighteen people from Jerusalem were killed and their families mourned their loss, because the builders did not lay a proper foundation for the Tower of Siloam. Those eighteen died, not because God lined up the worst sinners from Jerusalem and dropped the Tower on them like some type of divine mouse trap. They died in an unfortunate accident, because they were in the wrong place at the right time. We live in a dangerous world.

Murphree says,

Just as the abuse of moral freedom accounts for moral evil,

the abuse of natural freedom accounts for a large measure of
natural evil. Natural laws, as well as moral laws can be broken.
They may be inadvertently transgressed, but when they are
broken something happens somewhere.

For instance, a natural laws says two objects cannot occupy
the same space at the same time. When two approaching cars
on separate streets arrive at the same intersection at the same
time attempting to occupy the same space, something has to
give. A natural law says an object that is unrestrained will
move toward the earth. When the law of gravitation is transgressed, someone can get hurt.[64]

## Death From Disease

In the same regard, much physical suffering such as
disease, results from neglect of natural laws.

After a man in India lost a child in a cholera epidemic
he said, "Well, it's the will of God."

"Supposing someone crept up the steps onto your
veranda," the preacher said, "and deliberately put a wad
of cotton soaked in cholera germ culture over your little
girl's mouth. What would you think about that?"

"Who would do such a thing?" the Indian asked.
"Such a person should be killed. What do you mean by
suggesting such a thing?"

"Isn't that just what you have accused God of doing
when you said it was His will? Call your child's death the
result of mass ignorance, call it mass folly, call it mass
sin. If you like, call it bad drains or communal careless-
ness, but don't call it the will of God."

Surely, we cannot identify as the will of God something for which a man would be put into jail, or a mental
hospital.

## God Uses Suffering for Good

"As he [Jesus] went along, he saw a man blind from

birth. His disciples asked him, 'Rabbi, who sinned, this man or his parents, that he was born blind?'

"'Neither this man nor his parents sinned,' said Jesus, 'but this happened so that the work of God might be displayed in his life'" (John 9:1-3).

God knew that this boy would be born blind and sought to use it to His glory. But to say that God can make something good out of what has happened, is different than saying God made suffering happen so that good may come about.

God does not cause the suffering that results from disease or genetics, but once it is present He wastes no time in using it for good, if we let Him.

God does not desire suffering, does not cause it nor purpose it, but He can use it and make good come from it.

## A Loving God Cares About Those Who Suffer

Eventually, healing came to Skeeter's family but it took time, love, and teaching. Healing began when the grieving family experienced genuine compassion and love from Christians in the church. Seeing first the visible love of the church, they came to realize God's love and learned of God's will as well.

In one circumstance I felt compelled to comment at a funeral on the issue of death and the will of God.

Bruce was a 36-year-old man who was "as strong as a horse." He had a wife, two teenaged daughters and a son in fifth grade. They had just bought 47 acres and a new home in March. One Tuesday evening the end of July, Bruce had an intense asthmatic attack. It was fatal.

Bruce's young widow not only grieved his loss, but blamed God for taking her husband, especially at a time when she and the children needed him most.

This death sent shock waves through the whole community. Bruce was a popular and active member of the community. He was a member of the church, a volunteer firefighter, played on area softball teams, coached Pop Warner Football, coached Little League Baseball, and delivered fuel for the LaPorte County Co-Op.

The greeting line for viewing of the deceased ran the whole length of the funeral home and out into the street. Over a thousand people visited with the family that day.

My ties with the family had remained close even though I had left that congregation four years before.

When Bruce's mom called with the news, I told them I would drive to Indiana from Michigan to be with the family for the viewing and funeral. Whether or not I spoke at the funeral was not as important as being with the family. Bruce's parents, Les and Lois, had lost another son, Mark, years before and I knew how *that* loss still brought tears to their eyes.

When the family asked me to participate in the service, I struggled with what to say. I knew Brenda and others were asking, "Why did God take Bruce?" The issues were too involved to articulate every aspect, and the philosophical jargon seemed inappropriate for a funeral setting. I prayed for wisdom.

After the local minister opened with Scripture and prayer, "The Old Rugged Cross" was played at the largest funeral I had ever seen. I began the personal profile with the list of survivors, then spoke of Bruce's three primary characteristics — he was an Encourager, a Competitor, and a Friend. I illustrated each with stories and anecdotes about his wife, children, Christian friends, and told of the basketball and softball games in which we had played together.

I then addressed the issue of Bruce's *untimely* death in this way:

"Situations like today are a tragedy — a young man leaves behind a young family. . . On a difficult day like today we ask ourselves, 'Why? Why, did this happen?'

"We know the medical reasons why but we ask, 'Why?' seeking a purpose to this event. Some people may erroneously say to the family, 'Be comforted because this death must be the will of God.'

"I want you to know that death is not the will of God. God is not a puppeteer in heaven with strings on all our earthly lives, Who deciding *our time is up*, pulls on the strings jerking us out of this life into the next.

"God is not such a God.

"The God the Bible describes, and the Father of Jesus, is a God who loves you so much He gives you *freedom* to love Him because you choose to. Everything that happens in our lives is an interaction of our free choices and those of others. God has not appointed a specific time and moment for each person to leave this life. If He were such a God, I would have trouble with that presumption when someone is murdered. I would ask what kind of God would condone *that* kind of death, when even in His Word He says, 'Thou shall not murder.'

"So we have to be careful about simply, glibly covering everything by saying, 'This is the will of God.' Death is not the will of God. It was never the will of God for death. You remember the story of Adam and Eve in the Garden, don't you? There was a tree of knowledge of good and evil and God wanted *life* for His creation. But He said that the day you eat of that tree — the day you disobey Me with your freedom to choose — you shall surely die. The decay which lead to physical death began on the day they ate.

"It was not a part of God's will for death; God's plan for us is *life*. God is not simply snatching people away from us; He wants to love us and show us His direction.

"As a matter of fact, God loves us so much He gave us the freedom to reject Him or blame Him for the suffering we endure, because we think Him unloving or unpowerful. Think of the story of the Prodigal Son. The reason the father gave the younger son his inheritance (before the father died) was to give the son the freedom (that the money provided) to choose the father's will or to reject it. The son chose to run off to a foreign land, but later he 'came to his senses' and returned. When the father saw him on the horizon, he ran to his son, embraced him and welcomed him home.

"The father did not *cause* the suffering that the son endured, but when the son turned to the father for comfort, he received more comfort than he could have ever dreamed. . . ."

## Chapter 5

# First Hours... First Days

## "Standing By" Mourners

*I am worn out from groaning;*
*all night long I flood my bed with weeping*
*and drench my couch with tears.*
*My eyes grow weak with sorrow...* [69]
—King David

Whether a loved one dies by a sudden accident or after a long illness the death sends the shocked family into the Garden Maze of grief. We may assume that when a person dies after a prolonged illness, that the family would be more prepared for the final day. That is often not the case. Maybe it is because they have seen him recover so many times when they thought he was dying, that it shocks them when death finally does come.

Pain and confusion fill those first hours and days after a death as the mourners seek to come to grips with all the activities that follow. Friends and relatives begin to arrive. Flowers and plants are delivered. Friends bring dishes of hot food and offer a hug. As the funeral is planned, so many questions, memories, and feelings flash through their minds.

The grieving observe all the activity and go through the motions, yet somehow it all seems outside themselves, as though they are in a daze or a dream. But they know in their hearts that it *is* a reality. Here they stumble into the Signpost of Numbness and Denial. Here they need a friend to *stand by them*, to listen and assist them, and — when the grieving ask — to help them.

## First Hours of Shock and Numbness

Denial and numbness is the mind's way of coping with the intense shock and pain of having your whole world — and your future — torn apart by the death of someone you love. We say, "I cannot believe this has happened."

We are right. We *cannot* believe it.

At such times, *intellectually* we know that the loss has happened, but *emotionally*, we cannot come to grips with the event — "we're in shock."

We do not *want* to believe it.

Some people sob uncontrollably, others sit silently. Both are natural responses.

The natural tendency, however, is to worry more about the person who shows intense overt signs of grief — like passing out at the funeral, weeping intensely at the casket, or speaking with the body of the deceased. But such signs of overt grieving do not mean that a person will struggle continually. Murray Parkes' study indicates that those who grieve overtly at the beginning cope *better* in later months and years. Those who hold in their expressions of grief, will struggle more later.

> One of the important observations made as a result of the [Parkes'] study had to do with differences in the degree of the overt expression of emotional distress immediately following the loss and the longer-term outcome with regard to emotional adjustment. The group of widows with the mildest forms of emotional expression during the first week of bereavement grew to be the most disturbed in the third month. During the period of six to nine months it was impossible to distinguish them from the two groups who were moderately and severely disturbed initially.
>
> However, toward the end of the year the first group again became more disturbed, and after the end of the year, three out of the five widows in this group were now moderately or severely disturbed. In contrast, only one of eight widows who were in the initial severe-affect group were similarly disturbed. *It is difficult to avoid the conclusion that early full grieving, the overt exhibiting of emotional behavior, produces a reduction in later symptoms of disturbance, while the repression or covering up of initial affect leads to a greater severity of those feelings when they finally do emerge.*[70]

# Please, Stand By. . .

During those first few hours of grief, friends can assist the grieving with several physical needs. But well-meaning friends must not try to do everything for the mourners, nor to impose themselves and their opinions on them.

*Stand by* them, share with them, listen to them but let them make the arrangements and the decisions. Then finally, if they ask, answer questions carefully.

Mourners should continue as much of their usual activities as possible during the period of crisis. It is certainly not good for someone to take over completely and make all the decisions. Well-meaning relatives and friends can hinder the grief process by forcing the grieving to sit inactively by. This is much like the surgery patients in the past who were coddled and told not to do *anything* for several days after surgery. All that only prolonged the patient's sickness and required a longer recovery period.

A housemother of a large sorority at a Midwestern university says,

> I always make it a point to be right there near the girl the whole time she is making telephone calls and preparing to leave. But I always keep her as busy as I can, letting her do her own packing and making her own minute-to-minute decisions. The other girls in the house always want to wait on her hand and foot, but I've learned that this is the worst thing you can do for a person at such a time.[71]

Because the number of activities multiplies during times of crisis, friends can comfort the mourning by helping with the tremendous load of physical needs. The number of people in the home usually increase as family returns for the funeral; therefore the burden of cooking and cleaning is increased.

One lady took a hot ready-to-eat meal over the evening the loved one died, "because you need to eat now as well as the day of the funeral." Another lady brought a box of crackers and a large pot of chili, "so you *can* fix a quick bite when you need something in a hurry."

Sometimes a little cleaning helps too. On the day of the death of her husband, one lady fretted because all the friends and relatives came to visit her. She had not been able to clean her bathroom. Now when her friends lose a spouse she goes to visit, excuses herself to the bathroom and *cleans* it. She then returns to the grieving widow, hugs her, and whispers in her ear, "Don't worry, your bathroom is clean."

Another friend arrived at the home with a notebook, then proceeded to answer the phone, record accurate information, and relay messages. Precious phone calls were preserved. Later the family reviewed them, and each provided a measure of healing.

A prompt, short note sent immediately furnishes comfort too. Sending flowers and plants is a time-honored way to show compassion. Their color, fragrance, and beauty can become a physical sign of friends who care.

In the midst of this time the grieving are faced with several questions that they may or may not have discussed with the deceased.

"Do we want a funeral?" "Where will we hold the funeral?" "Who will speak?" "Should the casket be opened or closed?" "Should we bring the children to the viewing or the funeral?"

"What about cremation?" "If she is cremated, do we have a Memorial Service?" "Where can we spread the ashes, like she wanted?"

"Who is to make the funeral arrangements?"

# Making Funeral Arrangements

*Who makes the funeral arrangements?* The next-of-kin does. *Who then is the next-of-kin?*

Under the laws of most states the authorization of funeral arrangements can be made only by the next-of-kin. The wishes of the next-of-kin supersedes the expressed wishes of the deceased contained in the deceased's will or other written or oral communication. The only exception to this is if the deceased has arranged for his body to be donated to medical science, in which case, by statute, the deceased's wishes must be respected. The personal representative or executor of the estate has no special authority to make funeral arrangements contrary to the wishes of the next-of-kin.

Who is the next-of-kin? In general, next-of-kin are determined in the following order: Spouse; children; grandchildren; parents; siblings; nieces and nephews; grandparents; aunts and uncles; first cousins. If there are several next-of-kin within the same degree of kinship (for example, the spouse is dead and there are several children living), then most funeral directors will require that all the next-of-kin be in agreement before proceeding. The law has no provision for "majority rule." If problems reaching agreement are anticipated, it is best to work out an understanding or accommodation prior to death in order to avoid delays and legal entanglements once the death has occurred.[72]

# Standing By on Tough Days

The next-of-kin laws are being tested in unusual ways in our culture today. In Indiana for instance, a twenty-two-year-old homosexual, a son of a Christian couple, died of AIDS. His homosexual bedfellow organized the funeral and spoke at the service. He used the memorial service to promote that lifestyle and speak of AIDS issues.

Imagine the pain and horror of the Christian parents, as they had to sit through such a service, especially when they knew and saw such open rebellion to God's intended lifestyle and will.[73] Far too often the first question the Christian community asks when they find out about a rebellious child is, "What did the parents do wrong?" Many times the answer is, "Nothing." But we seek to find fault. We think that, "If we raise a child in the way he shall go he shall never depart." I agree, yet if we take that to the extreme we will really indicate, "If I raise my child properly, he will have no free will and will *have* to be saved. His salvation depends upon our perfection as parents." Such is, obviously, not the case. Every child's fate, no matter how well or poorly raised, will be his decision. God's grace of free choice is a difficult one.

Instead of looking for a place to lay fault, God has called us to comfort the grieving. To *stand by* them in their hour of crisis. In this case the couple's two ministers did attend the funeral, but then they stood up and marched out in the middle of the speech.

How sad.

I realize it must have been extremely difficult for them to sit there and listen to such rebellion. Maybe they thought that by sitting there they would in some way condone that lifestyle or speech. I do not know. I do know that when they left that couple *alone* they also walked out on what comfort means — *please stand by me. . .*

Christians will be increasingly faced with similar situations. How will we respond? In judgment? In fear? In love? In comfort?

The couple's ministers just told them, "Put his death behind you and get on with your lives." That statement trivialized their loss, their pain, and the death. They never went back to that church.

One lady from the church, however, kept in contact with the couple. She sent them cards and notes of encouragement, balloons, and flowers. Mostly, she just had the courage and compassion to *stand by* them. The mother sent several cards back to her Christian friend, stating how she bounced between feelings of sadness, illness, rejection, and anger, and how "your cards have meant so much to me and came *just at the right time.* I praise God that He gave me a kind friend like you, who listens without judging!"

"To listen is the first act of an empathic response. A mother, helping her daughter with word definitions, asked, 'What is the difference between *sympathy* and *empathy*?' The daughter thought for a moment and then said, 'Sympathy is what I feel when you hurt. And empathy is your pain in my heart!'"[74]

## Decisions of the First Days

In the first days of trauma and grief the mourning must make several important decisions that could have lasting effects for years to come. Fortunately, they have funeral directors who provide compassionate and professional assistance in many areas during this time. As we have mentioned, funeral directors (like ministers) receive a lot of misdirected anger from the grieving. Most of this anger is undeserved. Funeral directors provide answers and assist the survivors with organizing the funeral service, contacting speakers, organizing the clothes, obtaining death certificates, and answering questions about insurance, grave sites, markers, obituaries, memorials, and flowers.

The survivors must decide about embalming and/or

cremation, family and public viewing times, and plan the funeral service. During that time the questions can seem endless.

*Why have a funeral?*

This is a reasonable question. Funerals can be a catalyst for healing. A time to say, "Good-bye" to the deceased. A time to acknowledge our loss publicly and to recognize the significance of the deceased and what impact he had on our lives. Basically it is a time for closure.

A college student in a grief class talked about the need for the closure a funeral can provide,

> My mother died three years ago. I was going to remember her as she was, so I did not see her after her death. I would not go to the funeral home and barely went to the funeral. I would not allow myself to think about her or her death. I never did deal with her death until the night I graduated from high school. I was walking across the stage to receive my diploma and happened to see my father in the audience. Dad was sitting next to an empty chair, and my mother's death hit me. I fell apart right there on the stage. A few months ago my grandmother died. I went to see her body in the funeral home, it gave me closure. I dealt with her death.[75]

In *Healing Grief*, Amy Jensen advised survivors on the value of personalized funerals,

> Consider, however, that a service tends to benefit the survivors, most of whom will receive some healing from it. A funeral or memorial service can do more. It brings the support of friends and community. It gives you a goal, a stabilizing objective in those first uncharted, emotional days. And it provides for a last, loving tribute, a public declaration of love.
>
> Be involved in the planning if you can. Choosing music and speaker brings a sense of control and makes the service more meaningful. It is better to have an old friend speak with tears than an unknown clergyman speak with eloquence.[76]

I agree. But practically speaking, a minister is often the only spokesman. More on that later.

*Where should we hold the funeral service?*

Most funerals are held at funeral homes, but that need not be the case. My father-in-law's memorial service was held in the Sportsman's Club that he helped build. Many Christians have funerals in a church building. Having a service in a church building has its benefits and drawbacks. When my sister-in-law's brother died as a young man, his funeral was in her church. For some time thereafter Cheryl struggled with painful memories of her brother when she worshiped there. What had once been a place of joy and communion became a reminder of his casket and her loss. But not everyone has the same response. Others have found that having the service at the church building promotes healing especially when they return to worship there.

*Who will speak at the funeral?*

There are more options here then may appear at first glance. A minister, or two, may share in the service. A former minister may be called to return to share in the service. A friend or relative can speak at the funeral. We will cover the details about organizing the service in the next chapter. For now, remember that the funeral service becomes a catalyst for healing when we remember the deceased and acknowledge the hope — the assurance — of eternal life through the resurrection of Jesus Christ.

*Should the casket be opened or closed?*

Here is another area where the skillful hands of a funeral director can comfort the family. As the body is fixed up during embalming, the family need not remember the deceased in the deteriorating process of death.

Their last view may be much closer to what the deceased looked like.

Lois Duncan learned through painful experience why it is best to view the body. She followed her mother's desire for a closed casket and paid dearly for it.

> She [mom] told me the service would be short and the casket closed. "Grandma would want us to remember her as she was alive."
>
> Those words echoed in my mind as I arranged my own mother's funeral. I never saw my mother's corpse — and I never allowed anyone else to. When well-meaning friends began arriving at the funeral home to 'view the remains,' I was horrified. I insisted the casket be kept closed, the way I knew Mother would have wanted it. I was never totally convinced she was in it.
>
> Today — over fifteen years later — I still am not convinced. I have frequent dreams of receiving a telegram announcing that Mother has "finally been located" and that the report of a fatal heart attack was incorrect. I awake from those dreams confused. Then, as reality takes over, I am overwhelmed by a rush of pain as raw and all-consuming as it was on the day she died.[77]

*Should children view the body in the casket or go to the funeral?*

Should young children attend funerals or view the body? Some people believe they should not. But careful consideration should be given to each child because her grief and needs may be as great as an adult's, and her bewilderment will be even greater. Generally, children should not be forced to go, but let her look if she wants to and if she can understand a simple explanation of the circumstances.

Here is one mother's story,

> We were uncertain whether six-year-old Demeree should see her brother in the "slumber room." I told her she could come with the family and we would decide later. As we stood

around Michael's small casket, Demeree gradually crept forward and peeked. Quiet tears rolled down her cheeks. Later she said she should have brought her hankie. I mistakenly said, "I wouldn't have let you see him if I had known it would make you cry." "No," she replied, "I *wanted* to see him. I just wish I had brought my hankie."[78]

As we mentioned earlier, give children direct and simple answers about death.

Dr. Earl Grollman explains in *When Children Hurt,*

> Since so much depends upon each youngster's stage of development, the grieving process in children is highly complex. For instance, a three-year-old's understanding of death (and their mourning process) will be different from that of a six-year-old. Both will be dissimilar from a ten-year-old.
>
> The Hungarian psychologist, Maria Nagy, explored the meaning of death for children of various ages. She found at ages three to five, they deny that death is final. To them it is like sleep; like a parent going to work or on a brief vacation. Between five and nine, youngsters accept the idea that someone has died, but usually not until the age of ten do they understand that they themselves must die.
>
> Don't rush with explanations that children cannot understand, or play one big 'tell-it-all.' Thoughts must be translated into the comprehension of each child. Avoid abstractions by using simple and direct language.[79]

Children — as well as adults — have difficulty emotionally realizing a loved one is dead unless they see their body. Seeing the body confronts our denial. We may think that we are sheltering them from pain but the opposite is true, as Lois Duncan experienced.

> Their grandmother's death is not a reality to [my children]. Last Christmas, our youngest daughter bought Nana a present — "I saw this and I know how much she likes blue."
>
> Our teenage son, preparing to fly to Michigan for the wedding of a cousin, said, "I hope he brings Nana to the airport."
>
> "Honey, Nana is dead," I said gently.

"I forgot," he responded sheepishly.

Our children are not stupid. On an intellectual level, they know their grandmother is dead. On a emotional level, however, they "forgot." In their hearts, they harbor the belief that she is in hiding and will someday pop out, shouting "Surprise!"

I now believe that I did our children an injustice by not giving them the opportunity to come to grips with the death of their grandmother at her funeral. In my efforts to shelter them from pain, I may have left open an emotional door that they'll have to struggle for years to close. I do not intend to make the same mistake the next time a loved one dies.[80]

### *Do you want cremation?*

When the deceased or the survivors want the body cremated there are several ways to facilitate that with the memorial service. The deceased can be embalmed for the viewing and the funeral service but, instead of the graveside service the body is taken for cremation.

Cremation is becoming increasingly popular — some statistics show that the number of cremations may be nearing forty percent. Cremation reduces the body to small bone fragments, which are pulverized, reducing the fragments to the consistency of coarse sand or crushed sea shells. If the body is cremated before the viewing or memorial service, the family can organize pictures and other items to set near the urn, to remind the friends and family of the deceased.

Because my father-in-law requested to be cremated, children were called in to see Vic, before he was taken away from the home. Seeing him dead was the closure we needed to begin the healing process. His ashes were brought to the memorial service along with several personal items that reminded us of him.

The spreading of the ashes provided another time for the family to say good-bye and deal with the "body." This made the death real to each of us.

*What do we do with the ashes? Where can we spread the ashes?*

Spreading of ashes of a deceased is legal by most state laws. In Michigan, for instance, it is legal if you scatter them on private land, so long as scattering of cremated remains does not "interfere with the rights of others." The law makes no provision for scattering the ashes on public land or water. All rivers and most lakes in the United States are public property. Also it is legal to be buried at sea but no such provision enables people to be buried in the Great Lakes.

Following the memorial service for my father-in-law, we went to one of his favorite places to scatter his ashes. I found the experience very moving. After the family gathered in a circle and prayed, his wife took a handful of ashes then threw them. Each of us took a handful of ashes and scattered them. Even the grandchildren participated.

The location was meaningful because of its significance to him. It reminded me of him then and reminds me of him still. He was a fly fisherman, too. He taught me to fly cast and now I tie flies for fishing. Part of my memorial to Vic was to tie some special fishing flies and return there to toss them into the river.

Scattering the ashes is only one of the methods of disposition. The ashes may be buried in the earth, entombed in a mausoleum, or placed in a niche of a columbarium. Or, they may remain in the possession of the family in an urn.

## The Big Event

The funeral service is usually *the* event of the first days of grief. That service can be a tragic, hollow, trivial ceremony or it can be a stimulus for healing. It becomes a therapeutic time when it establishes the significance of the deceased.

*Chapter 6*

# A Memorable Memorial

## *Funerals — a Catalyst for Healing*

*The function of a funeral is not just to honor the deceased
but to aid survivors in purging themselves of grief.
Like other rites of passage –
graduations, weddings, retirement parties –
funerals help us adjust to major life transitions.*[81]
—Lois Duncan

Survivors express more anger, criticism, and anguish over funerals than anything else. In the same regard, funerals stimulate more healing than any other time. The funeral is a catalyst for action which can either heal or hurt.

Healing funeral services are those which are personalized to the deceased. Diana McKendree wrote of the benefits of funerals in *The Spiral of Grief*.

> The funeral service helps us focus on the person who has died, the life they led and the continuing impact they have on our lives. It is an opportunity to participate in a ritual and a rite of passage, which enables us to begin "letting go." Without this, our process of acceptance may be prolonged and difficult. As hard as it may be, seeing the body offers us the opportunity to say good-bye, helping to bring the relationship to a close.[82]

McKendree mentions the two primary reasons people attend funerals: to say good-bye to someone they love and to remember the impact of their relationship with the deceased.

*Personalized* funeral or memorial services focus on the same issues. They establish the significance of the deceased and the mourners' loss. When a service is personalized it becomes a catalyst for healing. *Impersonal* funeral services create only emptiness.

When my wife's grandpa McDowell died, we drove from Iowa to Michigan for his funeral. Because the

McDowells had no church affiliation, the funeral director had suggested a person to preside at the funeral. The
family had asked if I wanted to preach the message but
thinking I was too close to the situation, I declined.
After all, I needed comforting too.

At the funeral, the speaker finished in four minutes.
He mentioned Grandpa's name only once, in passing,
and read a "canned" prayer from a booklet. The family
was shocked. We felt hollow, empty, even cheated.
Stunned, we stood in a small group. As we gravitated
toward the casket, a pain which I did not understand
wrenched my stomach. My wife's eyes portrayed an
agony I had never seen before. Her eyes asked me to do
something, anything. . . .

I breathed a silent prayer, and asked the family to
gather in a circle. As we stood, arms intertwined in front
of the casket, I spoke of Grandpa and what he meant to
me. I mentioned the whitetail deer he shot — illegally —
out of his kitchen window while drinking his morning
coffee. I commented that he lied about his age to enter the
military and to serve in World War I. In China, during the
war, he fought "our guys," with boxing gloves in a ring.
Grandpa also held dozens of patents for his inventions and
he had traveled all over America collecting stones for his
Rock Shop. With tears, I recalled how he had given me
some of his tools. "Every man should have tools," he had
said. I acknowledged that I had the tools, but still could
not use them. Then I spoke of our pain and loss, then of
Jesus, who could heal our grief and give hope. I closed
with prayer and we left for the funeral dinner.

That day I learned, personally, of the comforting
power of stories. No one pretended that Grandpa was
perfect; we knew his faults and loved him anyway. I realized that personalized funerals need not be long nor
elaborate to be loving, effective, and comforting.

Personalized profiles of the deceased are not detailed biographies which include every part of his life from birth to death. Rather they are a recollection of the stories and details that sum up his life and remind the survivors of their relationship with him.

When the significance of the deceased and the loss of the grieving is neglected, the mourning become embittered. Manning wrote,

> Tom [my brother] liked funeral directors, he did not like funerals. His dislike was directed more to the clergy than anyone else. He did not like the impersonal sermons he heard. He complained that we clergy persons were more intent on conversion than on comfort. His criticism burned at first. After being out of the ministry for several years, I have found that clergy get more criticism about funerals than almost any other area.[83]

Ministers struggle more with personalizing the funeral service than any other aspect of grief ministry. Because time is so short between the time of death and the funeral itself, most would welcome help. I appreciate it when friends and family assist in making the service as personal as possible.

As we will see, friends of the family can help make funeral services personal and healing.

## An Impetus for Healing . . .
## Memories of the Deceased

After talking with hundreds of families I have learned that most families *want* to talk about their loved one and that sharing those memories can become a catalyst for healing.

When the family speaks of their feelings about the deceased, it guides them as they sort out their memories and put them into perspective. While the family shares their memories, a mother may realize how her son or daughter is coping with the loss. The reverse is often true.

After Bob Husted died his widow, Joann, called to ask if I would share with them at the funeral. I agreed and we set a time for me to visit with the family. The next evening I sat in the living room with Joann, the children, and one granddaughter. I told them I wanted to share a personal profile about Bob as a part of the funeral service and asked them to tell me about him. For two hours the family shared with me — and each other — what Bob had meant to them. They talked about his patience, his love, the items he made for them, and they even shared some humorous things he did. Each took time to dry their eyes as they spoke. Bob's significance and their loss was confirmed with each story they shared. The granddaughter shared how Grandpa had made her a radio out of spare parts. She cried as she mentioned how she had promised to bring it over for him to see again. But she never got the chance. As she cried, her grandmother and others hugged her while offering words of comfort.

After the funeral, the family sent a note.

"Thank you. . . The time you spent with the family Wednesday evening was appreciated by all and very therapeutic. Making the time you spent with us to assure that the service would be personal and meaningful was beyond our expectations. Thank you again."

I know of a friend of the grieving family who was not involved publicly in the funeral service, who talked with the family and wrote a profile of their loved one. The family gave it to the presiding minister, who read it as part of the service. As we will see, this could happen more often.

## An Overview of a Funeral Service

Each funeral service has three basic sections — the

introduction, the personal profile, and the sermon. The introduction examines the occasion of the funeral, the profile focuses on the deceased, and the sermon declares the assurance Christians have in Christ.

The following chart displays *one* of the many ways to outline a funeral service. Each part of the service can be personalized to create a service which heals.

**Overview of a Funeral Service**

*Introduction Section:*
> Special Music — song or instrumental
> Scripture Reading
> Introductory Paragraph
> List of Survivors
> Prayer
> Special Music — song or instrumental

*Personal Profile:*
> Biography of the Deceased
> Special Music
> Scripture Reading

*Sermon:*
> Assurance of Life in Jesus Christ
> Closing Prayer

*Introduction Section*

The introductory section examines the occasion of the funeral — "why we're here."

*Selecting Special Music.* Some families desire no special music, others desire congregational singing, and many request either instrumental music or that a song be sung. The family can personalize the music by choosing songs that were meaningful to the deceased or significant to the family. Before Luella Albee died of cancer, she had asked her teenaged granddaughter, Dawn Witt, to sing two songs for the funeral. Dawn had sung "Love Lifted Me" and "This World Is Not My Home" to her while Luella was bedridden. Because singing at the funeral was too emotional for Dawn, she recorded the songs on a tape and we played them as an introduction to the service.

*Selecting Scripture Readings.* The opening Scripture reading is usually a passage about God's comfort, Jesus, the resurrection or heaven — passages like Isaiah 40:1-8, John 14:1-6, Isaiah 61:1-3 and 1 Thessalonians 4:13-18. If the deceased had a favorite verse, it could be read to introduce the service.

*List of Survivors.* I encourage the reading of the list of survivors somewhere in the service, because it acknowledges their loss.

*The Personal Profile of the Deceased.* Next comes the biography of the deceased. The personal profile can be read by a family member, a friend, or by the presiding minister. It need not be long — just personal. The goal is to share personal details and stories to show the essence of the deceased's life — not give a play-by-play account of every year.

Special music or a Scripture reading can follow the profile and provide an introduction to the sermon to follow.

*Promise of Life in Jesus Christ.* The closing segment of the funeral is the sermon about the assurance of eternal life Christians have through Jesus. The presiding minister may choose to tell of a Christian deceased's faith and trust in Jesus.

## Making a Funeral *Personal*

There are several ways that a friend of the family, who is a non-preacher, can help make the funeral service a personal and healing time.

These ways include:

- encouraging the family to share their memories
- sharing your own personal memories
- writing a short personal profile of the deceased
- locate writings of the deceased that would comfort the family
- suggest ways to *personalize* the prelude and postlude songs, Scripture readings, congregational singing, and special music
- write a poem or create a "Memories Video."

Let's look at each of these ways.

## Encourage the Family to Remember

Of course, the most personal details about the deceased will come from their family. If they do write about their loss and their memories, then a friend or a relative can read it during the service. When Maxine Straw died, her daughter, Deanna Melius, wrote the following profile and her brother read it as part of the funeral service. Their preacher followed it with a funeral sermon, in which, he too included some personal details.

There is a kind of gouging primal pain in losing your mother. Something that rips at the very soul and foundation of your being. She, after all, is your fountainhead, your place of origin, your well-spring. But the wound rips even deeper when your mother is your best friend, your confidant, your counselor, your partner in hilarity.

The only salve, the only help for healing is to exchange the cold and piercing image of my mother's face in death, with the gentler, warmer images I have stored in my mind over the years. Like the one of her sitting in her favorite seat at the back of the pontoon, sipping her iced tea from her favorite mug and stopping her light chatter just long enough to say "Look, there goes old Charlie, showing off for us again," as the great blue heron lazily glides to a more private spot on the lake.

Another favorite image is the one of her seriously settling into her familiar stance, crouching over her croquet mallet, about to take deadly aim at my croquet ball. And mumbling something like, "I have to hit you, Squeak, or you'll be right down here after me."

One of my mother's most endearing qualities was her wit and sense of humor. She loved someone's definition of stress: "When your gut says, 'No' and you mouth says, 'I'll be glad to.'" Another quote she had written down on a note pad was, "It's what you learn after you know it all, that counts."

We had to go to Flint so many times for various reasons in the past few years, that we had created a wide plethora of traditions associated with the trip. One such tradition was that we always wore white slacks to see who could make it all the way to Flint without spilling coffee on their slacks. Needless to say, one of us would always spill the coffee. We would go into gales of laughter and stop at the usual rest area to clean up, while the one who did the spilling had to suffer the deriding and disparaging remarks of the other. . . .

Above all my mother was a rugged individualist but she was always a lady. She abhorred the vulgarity that has steadily crept into television and permeated our homes and families. In days gone by, as surely as I knew the sun would make its way to morning again, I knew as we turned out onto the road in front of my parents' home that I would see the window-framed image of my mother, leaning over to wave good-bye. The window is dark and empty now, but, Mom, tonight I'll stand in the window frame and wave you a last good-bye.

## Share Your Memories

Friends of the family can write up their memories or a poem of the deceased and share them with the family, who may have them read during the service.

In Joan Persinger's profile I mentioned this story which demonstrated the love between Joan and my oldest son, Micaiah.

At Church, my three-year-old son, Micaiah, would often sit with Joan. When she became too ill to come to Church he always asked about her. One day recently, when we passed their house Micaiah said, "Joan doesn't feel good. I'm going to make her something." He was thinking of chocolate chip cookies though he couldn't even turn on the oven. . . .

When JoAnn Little's Christian friend, Kay, in Florida died, JoAnn was not able to attend the funeral. So she wrote a poem simple called, "For Kay." The poem expressed JoAnn's love for Kay, Kay's personality, Kay's Christian witness and JoAnn's empathy for Kay's family.

My friend, Ray Merritt, has a wonderful aptitude for comforting grieving families by writing "Letters from Heaven." Ray writes these fictional letters as if they are from the Christian deceased's viewpoint from heaven. They are genuinely personal and at times very humorous. As a part of the funeral, either Ray reads it or a friend of the family reads it.

Humor becomes a healing balm for a funeral profile only if the humor flows naturally from the life of the deceased. Any other type of humor seems crass or even worse.

## Write a Profile of the Deceased

If the family would like to have a personal profile written of the deceased, but they do not feel comfortable with writing it, then a friend of the family could write their stories for them. Writing a profile of the deceased is not as hard as it may seem at first glance. Just listen to their stories, record them, then write them in a logical fashion.

You can create a personal profile by relating, rehearsing, and recalling. First you *relate* with the family by comforting them and being a friend. Next they *rehearse* memories, stories, and details of the deceased with you. Then, you *recall* those memories by writing them into a profile to be read at the funeral.

Gathering personal details may seem awkward, but it is easier when you realize that the family usually wants to talk about their loss and their loved one. For most mourners, verbalizing their memories helps them sort out their feelings. Most express feelings of sorrow, loss, and love.

One friend of a grieving family asked them if she could write a short biographical sketch of their father. She then sat and talked with the family while asking them some simple questions. She recorded notes of the details then later wrote the profile, which she gave to the family. They in turn had another friend read it during the service.

These times to visit with the family are best left very informal. When you talk with the family you can ask questions about five areas of the deceased's life: Personal, Professional, Family, Favorites, and Faith.

*Personal Traits:*

Begin with questions about personal details about his or her childhood and personality. Ask questions like, "What stories did he enjoy telling about his childhood?" If you get a story that begins with, "When I was a kid, I walked four miles to school through snow drifts up to my eyeballs . . . ," use it — many will recall him telling it.

Ask about where they lived, the house they grew up in, and their school/college activities. Ask about the deceased's relationships with her neighbors.

Also ask, "How would you describe what kind of person she was?" "Was she outgoing or reserved?" "Can you think of a story that shows that?"

*Professional Background:*

The second category of questions is professional details. Ask questions about his life's work, how he chose it, and his relationship with co-workers.

"What was the first job he ever had?" "Who did he work for next?" "What stories did he tell about working there?"

Also under the Professional category, ask about any volunteer work the deceased did: volunteer fire department, hospital visitation, service club, or children's home.

Question the family about the deceased's military service. Carol's grandfather McDowell — who fought in WWI in China and spent most of this time boxing in the ring with other servicemen — is one example of a military anecdote.

In one interview, I learned of one man who served in the Navy during WWII and slept on ship beside parts of the A-Bomb, which shook Japan and left an irrevocable mark on twentieth century history. In his profile, I mentioned it.

*Family Relationships:*

Next ask about the deceased's relationships with the family. When they give you a general statement like, "She loved her grandkids very much," ask how she *showed* her love for them. "What activities did she do with her grandchildren?" "Did she take them to the park?" "Did she have a special dessert she made for them?" "Did she make handmade Christmas gifts for them?"

In Tom McGovern's profile, this anecdote was read which described the relationship between Tom and his stepdaughter.

The love that Tom received is typified with this clipping

from the Herald Argus newspaper from earlier this month.

"They say to have a real father is one of the best joys in life for a girl. But I want to say, having a STEPFATHER like you, Pop THOMAS McGOVERN is better than anything in this world. HAPPY 28TH ANNIVERSARY to you, Mom and Dad. I love you both dearly.

Your Daughter,<br>Brenda Pierce"

*Favorites:*

Next ask questions about the deceased's favorite activities and items. Ask about the deceased's favorite songs, artists, poems, poets, books, and authors. If you know a favorite book or author you may be able to include a quote.

Ask questions about favorite activities such as hiking, skiing, sewing, knitting, fishing, hunting, boating, baking, and gardening. Ask questions like, "Did she enjoy gardening?" If you find that she loved to garden and often gave away her tomatoes to family and friends, then mention it. Most of the audience will remember eating her tomatoes.

*Faith:*

The fifth category of questions is about the deceased's faith in God. Of course, your questions here will depend greatly on whether or not the deceased was a Christian.

Ask about her favorite Bible verse, book of the Bible, and hymn. If you learn a Christian's favorite Bible verse, include it in your profile.

The first time Joan Persinger was in the hospital with cancer, her in-laws visited her. They wondered how they could comfort her. Instead they found that Joan comforted *them*.

"Everything will be fine," Joan told them. "After all we're just foreigners in a strange land. We're just passing through." In her memorial profile I read Hebrews 11:13-16 to which she had alluded.

Ask about church membership and their involvement in the church's body-life. "Did they lead worship, sing special music, teach VBS, or work on building churches?" Ask about the times they mentioned God, Jesus, the church, or heaven. In all these categories seek out details that will encourage the mourners.

## Find Writings by the Deceased

Another source for details that create a personalized funeral service is the writings of the deceased. Ask the family if the deceased had written anything that would be appropriate to have read during the service, such as poetry or even a letter to a family member.

These writings of the deceased and of the family can offer encouragement and comfort to the mourners. For Clarence MuCullough's profile I read a recent letter sent to him from his son in California. It illustrated their relationship and the son's love for his dad.

In Katie Wild's profile, I read her poem "Smiles" which showed her attitude about life and encouragement. I also quoted some stanzas of Katie's poem called "Time," which warned us to make the most of our time for Jesus.

## Other Ways to Personalize a Funeral

There are several other ways to personalize funeral services. With the current popularity of video cameras, "Memories Videos" are appearing more often at funerals. Memories Videos contain pictures and scenes of the deceased with the family. Some of these are masterfully done and share many memories with the family and friends.

More often the family brings in pictures of the deceased along with other items that were meaningful to her or the family. This activity seems especially important during the services where the deceased was cremated and there is no "viewing." After my father-in-law was cremated — as he requested — the family brought several items and lots of photographs of him to the memorial service. These items seemed particularly meaningful to those in attendance.

The selection of the background music can comfort the grieving too. One lady was very active in a dulcimer society and played for area bands. For her prelude and postlude music they played dulcimer music. For special music during the service they played a Christian hymn that she had played on the dulcimer.

The selection of congregational songs can personalize the funeral service. At my funeral, I want them to sing "Love Lifted Me," and "Wonderful Grace of Jesus."

During the months that Joan Persinger struggled with cancer, her *favorite* hymn was "It Is Well With My Soul," by Horatio Spafford. Surprisingly, that hymn was written after Spafford had lost all of his daughters to a storm at sea. Later, as he sailed across to Europe, he wrote these words when the ship neared the spot where the storm had taken his daughters.

> When peace like a river attendeth my way,
> When sorrows like sea-billows roll,
> Whatever my lot, Thou hast taught me to say,
> "It is well, it is well with my soul."

## A Personalized Committal Service

Even graveside services can be personalized. Judy Phillips' committal service was personalized by mentioning that she had often sung special music for church and reading two verses of one of her favorite hymns, "Beyond The Sunset."

Note Judy's comforting words to the family as expressed through this hymn:

Beyond the sunset, O blissful morning,
  When with our Savior heaven is begun.
Earth's toiling ended, O glorious dawning;
  Beyond the sunset, when day is done.
Beyond the sunset, O glad reunion,
  When our dear loved ones who've gone before;
In that fair homeland we'll know no parting,
  Beyond the sunset, for ever more!

Personalized funerals are a catalyst for healing, but grief and mourning do not end at the graveside. Your friendship and comfort are especially needed in the days and months to follow.

# Chapter 7

# After the Funeral

## Comforting That Continues

*One winter they lost their son*
*but the pain didn't leave them crippled*
*and the scars have made them strong.*
*Never picture perfect*
*just a plain man and his wife. . .*
*They tried to give faith hands and feet*
*and somehow gave it wings . . .*[84]
Never Picture Perfect — Rich Mullins

Mourning does not end at the graveside but too often the comforting does. In the weeks and months that follow a death, the grieving process continues, but the overwhelming flood of encouragement that swept in for the funeral slows to a trickle.

A house, once bubbling with relatives and friends, becomes a collection of silent rooms. Sympathy cards no longer arrive with the morning mail. The grieving return to work and daily schedules, but the pain continues though it is easier to control the tears. Months, even years later, sorrow surfaces when survivors encounter another Signpost of Grief. These times of renewed mourning often result when the survivors are confronted with reminders of the deceased, such as his favorite flower, food, song, or hymn. Special days — birthdays, Christmas, anniversaries, Memorial Day, Mother's Day — are often moments of renewed loss and mourning.

Mourning does not end at the committal service, but far too often ministry does.

In *The Minister as Crisis Counselor*, David K. Switzer wrote,

> In a pilot study, one community service took the initiative in contacting 20 bereaved families, eight days after the death of a family member, to offer their counseling services. The stated assumption of the agency was that the persons' usual sources of support would be inadequate at this particular time. The fact that 18 of the 20 families accepted the offer is proba-

bly some kind of judgement upon the ministry of the area.[85]

Fortunately, there are ways to keep comforting after the funeral. The ministry of Christians comforted Marjorie Gordon, after the accidental death of her 25-year-old son, David. She wrote, "The days, weeks, and months that followed were bearable only because many friends touched us with their care, love, and prayers. We were like the little boy who was afraid of the dark. . . ."[86]

As we will see, this comforting ministry is easier than it may seem. The chief qualification? Concern.

Sometimes those who are grieving a loss find strength to keep going through ministering to others in grief. They "comfort others with the comfort God has given them."[87] Karen's seventeen-year-old son, Joey, died in an auto accident when his friend swerved to miss a deer and struck a bridge abutment. At the public viewing, Karen sat stoically. Many people tried to comfort her with words and hugs. They said, "We're really sorry." "Is there anything we can do?" Some even said, "We understand what you're going through."

Karen did not cry. She knew they did not understand.

Later, Karen's neighbor, Annette, came into the viewing room. When their eyes met, Karen stood up for the first time. They embraced, neither spoke. They sat and cried.

Karen had received many hugs that day, but this was a hug of identity. Karen knew, without a word, that Annette understood her pain — Annette had lost her son to cancer seven months earlier.

I never understood many of the aspects of grief until I lost my father-in-law, Vic Bierschbach. He was more than a father-in-law, he was my friend. We traveled on many fishing trips together. He taught me fly-fishing, gave me my first fly-rod, and was a subject of my magazine articles on the topic. Losing him allowed me — rather reluctantly — to "sit where the people sit." Now, when others lose a parent I can better understand. In their eyes I can see my own pain.

*Grief and mourning do not end at the funeral.* Recent studies attest that some of the oldest funeral traditions may be the wisest. One such tradition was that a widow could wear black for a whole year after her husband's death. This visible sign reminded everyone that her grief did not end in six weeks.

In his book David Switzer commented on a study entitled, "The First Year of Bereavement," written by C. Murray Parkes. He wrote about the duration of the grieving process,

> A summary of the situation after thirteen months showed loneliness still to be a very common problem. Social adjustment was rated by the interviewer as good in five instances, fair in nine, poor in eight. Six widows had definitely worse health than before the death of their husbands, and none was healthier. Six reported themselves as happy, seven as sad, two as neutral, and seven as having moods that fluctuated between happiness and sadness. In terms of overall adjustment, the interviewer made the judgement that three were very poorly adjusted, depressed, and grieving a great deal, nine were intermittently disturbed and depressed, six showed a tenuous adjustment which might be easily upset, and four had made a good adjustment. The conclusion is that even after thirteen months, the process of grieving was still going on, and although all the principle features were past their peak, there was no sense in which grief could be said to have finished.[88]

Often the *firsts* of that year, like his birthday, their anniversary, and holidays, become intense days of mourning. Katie and Rayford Wild shared many activities together. Each December they traveled to the Department of Natural Resources' check station for opening day of elk season. After her death, he asked me to go with him that December. Knowing what a rough "first" this would be for my friend, I agreed.

On the way home that day we stopped for dinner at one of Katie's favorite restaurants. Over dinner, we talked about Katie and how much she enjoyed days like this one with Rayford. This rugged outdoorsman cried and spoke of her with warmth and love. Clearly that day became a stepping stone to overcome his grief and remember Katie with love. That experience has taught me that grief comes in waves on the survivors and that a comforting hand on those days can save them from being swept out with the tide.

> A typical illustration was the experience of a widow whose husband died a year or so ago who is with a group of friends who knew her husband. As they are talking together, one of them recalls a very humorous story about her husband. He is about to tell it, and then he thinks to himself, "Oh no, I must not reopen the wound. I must be considerate of her." Consequently he carefully steers away from any conversation about her husband, as does everyone else. Actually, if he had told this story, she doubtless would have laughed heartily and been most pleased. He might have seen a tear or two in her eyes. If he had said, "I'm sorry. I should not have told that story," her response in all probability would have been, "Don't say that! You are the first person in weeks who has even mentioned my husband. No one ever talks about him any more. It is a wonderful feeling to know that someone still remembers him."
>
> Most people who are grieving are very considerate of others. They do not wish to force their troubles on other people.[89]

## Ways Comforting Can Continue

### *Keep On Listening*

Listening to the mourners now may be more important than earlier, because there are less opportunities for them to express their grief. Mourning people want to share about the deceased. They are hurt when friends treat the deceased's name as taboo, or say, "You should have been over this in three months. Put it behind you and go on."

One mother, whose son took his own life just before Christmas, wanted someone to listen to her. To find someone, she had to turn to a support group of other suicide survivors. She said,

> Just talking with and hearing from people who have gone through the same thing was a tremendous help and made me feel normal again. One of the things which was particularly helpful was that we survivors read the letter left behind. Before I joined the support group, I wanted to read my letter and talk about it, but no one wanted to hear it. But people who have gone through this know how important that is and we are willing to listen and share.[90]

Marjorie Gordon also wrote of the importance of listening,

> To be a comforter — a mourning partner — you don't need to give friends answers. Sit with them, pray with them, walk with them, wait with them. If they ask the inevitable "Why?" your response can be, "I don't know why, but I'll stay with you."
>
> Listen when the story is told over and over. . . . Don't attempt to solve the problem. Remember the mourning process takes a long time.
>
> Some people who feel inadequate to meet another's needs respond by withdrawing. They add to the hurt without knowing it. Their friend is thinking, *Why haven't I heard from him or her?*[91]

## Remember Special Days

During the first year after a death, several special days will renew the grief of loved ones. Marjorie Gordon wrote,

Write about a special moment. Like medicine for our broken hearts were the letters from Dave's friends. Many were from people we hadn't seen in several years. Some we had never met. Each searched to get our new address. Word pictures beginning, "I remember when Dave and I . . ." recounted special moments that brought laughter and tears as we read them.

The tenderness of warmhearted friends helped us on difficult days throughout the year following our loss. . . . My uncontrollable tears on Dave's birthday were punctuated with phone calls.

On Mother's Day I received a phone call from a friend who visited David's grave that day in the Black Hills National Cemetery in Sturgis, South Dakota. He knew we lived 1,100 miles away. "I wanted to tell you there was a fresh-cut red rose in a bud vase and a potted plant with lavender blossoms at Dave's headstone when we arrived." He will never know how important his message was.[92]

Mother's Day, birthdays (both the deceased's and the survivor's), wedding anniversaries, family reunions, Christmas, Thanksgiving, Easter, and the date of the death, all bring with them a renewed sense of loss.

Jean Schaefer in "Beyond Sympathy," *Woman's Day*, writes,

First holidays. These are also difficult times for the recently widowed woman. The first Christmas without her husband, the first time his birthday comes around, are all likely to be bad days. Help her over them with a phone call, an invitation, a visit or a warm note.

Sunday. Your friend may dread these traditional family days the most. If she's living alone, take her to church and home for brunch. If she has young children, make a Sunday easier by including them in a backyard cookout or a trip to the zoo with your family.

## Send Notes and Letters

Your own expressions and words in a note or letter

may not be as eloquent as a poem on a sympathy card, but they mean more to the grieving. Notes containing memories of the deceased are often read and reread by the survivors. Phone calls can uplift the grieving on days of sadness, but do not let them replace personal letters.

Personal letters are important in the New Testament. If Luke and Acts were written to Theophilus, and if we include Paul's personal letters to Timothy (two), Titus and Philemon, and the letters of John to "the chosen lady" (2 John) and Gaius (3 John), then over half of the New Testament by volume and eight of the 27 books were written from one Christian to another. Though none of these epistles were written specifically to comfort the mourning, they lift personal letter writing to a higher level. Billions are still reading these letters.

Marjorie Gordon wrote of this important ministry,

> Prevent an empty mailbox. For the first three weeks the mailbox held its daily treasures of comfort — an anticipated refreshment for days still bathed in grief. It was painful when that first supply ran dry.
>
> But there were sensitive friends who knew this was the time to send a booklet, poem, or Scripture verses with some added words of encouragement. Once again, "I'm thinking of you" means so much. . .
>
> Two devoted friends sent weekly messages of hope. Letters of comfort arrived through the passing months. It's never too late to write.[93]

One lady sends notes on the anniversaries of wedding, birthday, and death. She writes a little note to say that she is thinking of the person during this time. She remembers much longer than most of us would think necessary. Remember there is no going back — no one is ever the same — we cannot go back to the way things were. She says that the notes that did the most good are the ones sent on the fourth, fifth, and sixth anniversaries of birthday and death. The grieving person still hurts on those days and has no idea that anyone still remembers. But this shy little lady does, and her remembering helps.[94]

## *Remember That Children Mourn Too*

Sometimes the overlooked survivors are the children affected by the death of a relative or friend.

Children are especially at risk when it is one of their siblings who died. Elizabeth Richter, author of a book on sibling grief entitled *Losing Someone You Love* wrote, "In the past several years, experts have begun to look at the emotional impact that sibling death has on sisters and brothers — and many are finding that adolescence may be the worst time of life for grief.

"'If I had to pick the family member at greatest emotional risk when a child dies,' says Gerald Koocher, staff psychologist at Children's Hospital in Boston,

> it would be the adolescent sibling. It's a period when a young person is going outside the family to establish himself as an individual within a peer group. They are trying very hard to escape the family unit. It's not a time when most kids want to sit down with their folks to talk about feelings."[95]

Young children may want to express their love and grief in unusual ways. Sometimes it is best to understand and aid them as they work through their grief. Mayo Mathers told eleven-year-old Landon's story in an article entitled "A Letter For Luke."

Landon told his mom one day, "I wish I could write a letter to Luke." The mother could see the tears her son was trying not to shed. Nine months before, Landon's friend, Luke, had died suddenly of a brain hemorrhage.

Landon's grief was deep, unreachable. His mother

longed to ease his pain, though she could do nothing except hold him as he wept. Maybe, she thought, writing a letter was a good idea. She handed Landon paper and colored pencils. "Tell Luke how much you miss him and how much you love him. Tell him you haven't forgotten him."

Landon wrote the letter. A long one. The completed paper was a work of art. He wrote each line in a different color and carefully drew an elaborate border around the edge. It was a love letter . . . a message from earth to heaven.

Landon folded the paper carefully, tied it to a balloon, and took it to a steep butte. Before they released it, they prayed that God would take it and give it to Luke. When the balloon disappeared through the clouds, Landon whispered reverently, "Did you see that, Mom? God got my balloon."[96]

## *Writing Helps Adults Too*

Writing gets our feelings out — both good and bad. Once those fears are put down in black letters on white paper, they do not look so devious or destructive. Grief writing can take the form of poetry, like the elegies of Appalachia which are published in local newspapers. Grief writing can also take the form of journal prose, like C.S. Lewis' *A Grief Observed*.

Lewis observed,

> This is the fourth — and the last — empty MS. book I can find in the house; at least nearly empty, for there are some pages of very ancient arithmetic at the end by J. I resolve to let this limit my jottings. I *will not* start buying books for the purpose. In so far this record was defense against total collapse, a safety valve, it has done some good. The other end I had in view turns out to have been based on a misunderstanding. I thought I could describe a *state*; make a map of sorrow.

Sorrow, however, turns out to be not a state but a process. It needs not a map but a history, and if I don't stop writing that history at some quite arbitrary point, there's no reason why I should ever stop. There is something new to be chronicled every day. Grief is like a long valley, a winding valley where any bend may reveal a totally new landscape. As I've already noted, not every bend does. Sometimes the surprise is the opposite one; you are presented with exactly the same sort of country you thought you had left behind miles ago. That is when you wonder whether the valley isn't a circular trench. But it isn't. There are partial recurrences, but the sequence doesn't repeat.[97]

The elegies of Appalachia are a tradition in the mountains. Coal miners, loggers, professors, farmers, social workers, pensioners, doctors, and others all pen elegies when they suffer a loss. *The Athens Messenger* in Athens, Ohio, publishes them in the classified ads section of the paper. People search for these grief poems under the "In Memoriam" or "Card of Thanks" sections.

In "Elegies in Appalachia," Michael Bugeja wrote,

On Sundays, the *Messenger* publishes as many as a dozen elegies, and I always turn to that section first. The poems come in all forms — rhymed, free verse, even prose paragraphs — whose sole purpose is to soothe (rather than impress).

Nonetheless, I am impressed by many of the poems. One in particular caught my eye. I found it about a year ago, addressed to my old friend, Ann Howland.

An elegy should honor the deceased person and comfort or inspire the living. . .

Ann believed in telling the truth. She loved words because she knew their power to heal pain and to help us carve paths to each other.

And that's exactly what elegies do. Many people who have claimed to get no pleasure from poetry have found themselves moved to write elegies when a loved one dies. Then they put their laments in a drawer or Bible and go back to disliking poetry. . . .[98]

Bugeja goes on to explain that the poem he found written to his friend, Ann, was written by her husband, Gerry. He was moved to write it months after her death when he found himself surrounded by the things that Ann most cherished — their farm, the horses, and their beautiful vista. Gerry said, "But I wrote an elegy not so much for Ann, but for her friends and patients [she was a psychologist]. She cared so much about each one that I thought we might share the loss."

Bugeja also stated that the best elegies had symbols associated with the deceased and a direct, descriptive or introspective voice. They are hopeful instead of hopeless, even though the Greek word for elegy means, "song of mourning." Whether they find a new appreciation for poetry or go back to disliking it, the elegy still works its healing power to "heal pain and to help us carve paths to each other."[99]

## Caution Quick Decisions

Delores Bius offers some sound advice for mourners who desire to make radical changes in their lives while they are still in grief.

Advice is rarely appreciated by anyone, but usually a bereaved person is more apt to seek it and listen to it. They might be cautioned that it is usually unwise to make any radical changes in residence, occupation, investments, or life-style for at least a year.

Far too often a widow or widower will sell the home and relocate in another state or move in with a child, only to regret it later. Likewise, if the deceased leaves the survivor well off financially, he or she is soon beset by salesmen or family members, all seeking a sale, investment, loan, or gift.

One widow whose husband died in our hospital was urged by a sister in another state to come and live with her. Heeding our advice, she first made a visit to her sister before deciding to sell her house. When she returned, she thanked us, saying,

131

"I discovered I liked neither the climate nor being with my sister twenty-four hours a day!"[100]

## Grief Recovery Support Group

The Hospice organization, local churches, funeral directors or hospitals can often direct the grief-stricken to grief support groups in the area. There is some solace in sharing with others who are struggling with the same pain, at the same time. In an Eastern legend a woman asks why she should have to bear such sorrow. To get her answer she had to go find a house which had not been touched by grief and return with a stone from that house. As she went to each house in the village she found that every home had a story of loss to tell. In consoling their sorrow she found strength for her own grief.[101]

## Healing Through Helping Others

My falconry friends, Charles and Gayle Williams, lost their young daughter Heather to leukemia, and they found strength through her memories and by helping others in need. Charles wrote about Heather:

> Heather was a bird watcher at heart. She must have had ten or more types of bird books. She especially loved the pictures and stories of hawks, but she loved all birds. . .
>
> Each year since Heather's death we hold a memorial picnic at my home, and many children with cancer attend. This year thirty-one families came to fish, play and ride horses and covered wagons, talk to clowns and see each other in an atmosphere other than the hospital. It's great for them and it does my family good to see them having such a fun time.
>
> They also like very much to see my hawk. Most of them have never seen a bird of prey, other than in a zoo, and sad to say, some will never see another in this life. For each year some don't make it back to the next year's picnic.

Some of you may have seen us on the Danny Thomas special entitled, "One More Day." The Heather in the movie is the Heather I'm speaking of. She was a beautiful child and a brave one in the end.

And yes, falconry and the many friends I have made in this sport have helped me tremendously to deal with mankind's greatest loss, for she is the wind beneath my wings.

Heather, I got you a hawk![102]

# A Lasting Thought

If we use all the techniques mentioned in this book, we will share eloquent stories of the deceased, but if we have not love, we will be as a clanging gong. The most comforting touch of all is the love of God. May they see Christ's compassion in our actions, and the Father's comfort in our eyes. May we become the channel through which God's love flows and His comfort graces their lives.

# Chapter 8

# Learning to Say Good-Bye

## Preparing Others for Our Own Death

*Though I walk through the valley of the shadow of death,*
*I fear no evil; for You are with me.*[103]
—King David

*Death is an experience of the whole person —*
*physical, emotional, spiritual, and practical dimensions —*
*each dimension must be an integral part of preparation as well.*[104]
—Albert Walsh

Often one of the greatest concerns of the terminally ill is those they will "leave behind." The dying worry about how the survivors will cope with their death. They wonder if they can somehow prepare them for the uncharted course they will travel.

Terminally ill Christians desire to comfort their friends and family by sharing their assurance of the resurrection in Christ. Everyone has *personal* loose ends to cope with, like personal experiences and memories to share with others, old emotional wounds to heal, and unsettled relational accounts to mend. Everyone also has *practical* loose ends to tie up, such as gathering personal documents like insurance papers, cemetery documents and birth certificates, and preplanning funeral and burial details. All of this will not only prepare the survivors for living and coping with their loss, but will allow the dying to die with peace because they "did everything they could."

## A "Win–Win" Situation

When Christians greet death with the assurance that it is not the end but the beginning, they pass on a legacy of faith the touches their survivors. When I visited with Ray Wild at the hospital before his risky multi-by-pass heart surgery, we prayed for the success of the operation. After the prayer, Ray said, "Kenn, you know I'm in a 'Win–Win' situation. If the surgery is a success, I win.

And if I die on the operation table, I *still* win."

That's assurance.

That's faith in Christ.

Before Ray's wife, Katie, died of cancer she had passed on her legacy of faith to her family and friends. They all told stories of how Katie shared her hope and assurance of heaven. She used what Gary Smalley calls an "emotional word picture" to speak about heaven to her son.

Grant once asked, "Mom, what is heaven like?" Katie replied, "Do you know what it's like when you're running the ball in a football game and the crowd is yelling and cheering?" "Yes," Grant replied. "Then you cross the *goal line* and everyone mobs you?" "Yes," he said. Then Katie said, "That's what heaven is going to be like."

Christian history abounds with stories of those, both famous and uncelebrated, who have shared their assurance of heaven with family and friends. Evangelist Dwight L. Moody once said, "One day you will read in the obituaries that, 'DWIGHT L. MOODY is dead.' When you do, don't you dare believe it. Because I will never be more alive than on that day!"

When Moody was on his deathbed in the hospital, his family had gathered at the doctor's request. The doctor took the family from his room and told them that Moody was slipping quickly.

They went back into his room and prayed by his bed for healing. When Dwight realized what was happening he said, "Don't pray that for me today. This is my Coronation Day!"

Speaking of her hope, Patricia Riesenweber shared an emotional word picture about her little brother and "the door."

One day when I was 13, I was taking my three-year-old

brother David to the church where my father was the minister. Mother had sent us to bring Dad home for lunch. To reach his office we had to pass through the church basement, a very dark and spooky place, and just before we came to Dad's door, I thought up a little prank.

"I'll plant David in front of the office door, knock boldly, the quickly run around the corner out of sight," I thought. "Dad will be expecting an adult and how surprised he'll be to see little David standing there."

I knocked on the door, and darted away. As I peeked around the corner, I could hear Dad's footsteps coming, yet through the gloom I also saw David's lower lip trembling. Only then did I realize what I had done to him, how frightened he was standing there alone in the big, scary basement, abandoned by his sister, listening to the heavy footsteps coming closer. Just then the door opened and he looked up into his Dad's face. David radiant with relief and joy, smiled and held up his arms. His Dad lifted him up and hugged him.

I often recall that moment when I think about death. If ever I'm frightened about facing that door alone, I simply imagine the joy I'll feel when the door opens and I look up into my Heavenly Father's face.[105]

In his March 1992 letter Dr. James Dobson shared his father's words about the legacy of faith that James' grandparents left.

At five minutes to four o'clock the nurse came in and awakened one of my twin brothers, [who] roused with a start. "Is he gone?" he asked.

"No, but if you boys want to see your dad one more time while he is alive, you'd better come, now."

At three minutes to four o'clock, like a stately ship moving slowly out of time's harbor into eternity's sea, he [Dad] breathed his last. The nurse motioned us to leave, and pulled the sheet over his head, a gesture that struck terror to my heart, and we turned with silent weeping to leave the room. Then an incident occurred that I will never forget. Just as we got to the door, I put my arm around my little mother and said, "Mama, this is awful."

Dabbing at her eyes with her handkerchief, she said, "Yes,

Jimmy, but there is one thing Mother wants you to remember, now. We have said 'good night' down here, but one of these days we are going to say 'good morning' up there."

I believe she did say "good morning" too, eleven years later, and I know he met her "just inside the Eastern gate."[106]

Dr. Dobson follows his father's words with his own story how that legacy of faith brought him consolation at his father's death.

A few years after dad penned those words, he was suddenly seized by a heart attack and lay dying in a Kansas City hospital. I rushed to his side and found myself experiencing that strange return to childhood of which he had written. As he had done for his father so many years before, I patted his old hand in an inexpressible moment of appreciation. Though he was a big, rugged man, 6 feet 4 inches tall, he had delicate, artistic fingers. He had used those hands to teach me how to cast with a rod and reel, and how to shoot a rifle, and how to draw and paint. I had seen him hold a King James Bible at least ten thousand times, thoughtfully turning the pages as he studied the Word. Soon, those beloved hands would be folded across his chest in stillness. It was an unbearable thought.

What incredible consolation there is in knowing, however that my little grandmother was right. While we must say "good-bye" down here to all that is cherished and familiar, we will someday say "good morning!" on the other side. And I believe the glorified body we will inherit will be recognizable from our days here on earth. We will see and hold our loved ones again in that dawn of eternity! We will feel the touch of those familiar hands![107]

John Quincy Adams offered this insight on the Bible statement "the outer man is decaying, yet the inner man is being renewed day by day."[108] One day in his eightieth year Adams was tottering down a Boston street. He was accosted by a friend who said, "And how is John Quincy Adams today?"

The former president of the United States replied graciously, "Thank you, John Quincy Adams is well, sir, quite well, I thank you. But the house in which he lives at present is becoming dilapidated. It is tottering upon its foundations. Time and the seasons have nearly destroyed it. Its roof is pretty well worn out, its walls are much shattered, and it trembles with every wind. The old tenement is becoming almost uninhabitable, and I think John Quincy Adams will have to move out of it soon; but he himself is quite well, sir, quite well." And with this the venerable statesman, leaning heavily upon his cane, moved slowly down the street.

John Quincy Adams had the same assurance which we all have. He knew that "if the earthly house of our tabernacle be dissolved, we have a building from God, a house not made with hands, eternal, in the heavens." (II Corinthians 5:1).[109]

## Personal Loose Ends

Besides sharing faith in Christ the dying also desire to tie up the loose ends in their lives. Everyone has memories that he needs to express to friends and family. These may be feelings on his heart that he could never share with them. He thought some day would come when he would share those thoughts. But the dying man soon realizes that those days never arrived. As he sees the end coming, he wants to find some closure for those relationships.

Albert Walsh wrote,

> When we make preparations for a trip we always find ourselves deciding what to take with us and what to leave behind. By analogy, the baggage may be memories of the times and personal experiences shared with others, old emotional wounds in need of healing, animosities and unsettled relational accounts, or even more tangible items such as letters to be shared, pictures to be given away, or items which hold great personal value (e.g., a watch, piece of furniture, etc.). These things, emotions, and situations can either be left behind or taken with us. We are stretching the analogy, because in our preparations for a trip we do not leave things behind for

others to possess. But remember that the analogy provides us merely with clues and should not be considered a one-to-one correlation. Death, because of its finality, gives this aspect of preparation a new meaning.[110]

In her book, *How To Get Along With Difficult People,* Florence Littauer shared how she had wanted to hear her aging mother tell her words of approval. Her mother's personality did not allow for such overt expressions of approval. Finally Littauer found the closure she needed by seeking to meet her mother's needs.

> I asked myself, "What does my mother need in her waning years?" She needs to know that she's important and that she's not been thrown into that large elderly wastebasket. What does my telling her about my trips do for her? It makes her feel older and of little significance. It in no way builds her up. It makes the difference between our lives — mine exciting and adventurous, hers dull and sedentary — even greater. I was approaching her all wrong. I was looking for the mother to praise the little girl when I should have been seeking to build her self-esteem.
>
> As I stopped talking at her and began listening to her, I gained a new respect for her attitude. One day she said, "I guess my life has been hard, but I've never looked at it that way as I was going through it."
>
> Another day as I asked her to tell me about her feelings for the retirement home in which she was living, she smiled and said softly, "They've put me at the head of the table and I'm the only one who had a chair with arms on it."
>
> Here I had been trying for years to get her excited over the size of my chair, and all she had wanted was for someone to put her at the head of the table in a chair with arms on it.[111]

That time of closure and acceptance allowed Littauer to better cope with her mother's death.

> The last evening I spent with Mother, as the cancer had brought her from 130 pounds down to 93, she said, "I'm so grateful I don't have any pain. So many of the ladies here are

in constant pain, and many are crippled and can't walk. I'm comfortable. I'm just tired."

The next day . . . She cut the tags off the new nightgown that my son had given her for Christmas . . . She put it on, went to sleep, and never woke up.

At the funeral my two brothers and I gave eulogies of what Mother's sweet and gentle spirit had meant to us, and I was able to say, "All she wanted was to sit at the head of the table and have a chair with arms on it, and now we know that she is seated at the right hand of the Father, and He has surely given her a big chair with arms on it."[112]

## Practical Loose Ends

We plan for every aspect of life such as family vacations, weddings, and retirement. We prepare for what *might* happen such as fires and accidents, but we often avoid making decisions about very practical things concerning our death, which will certainly happen.

As a result family members are often faced with difficult decisions in a time of grief, confusion and pain. They do not know what the deceased preferred and have to scramble to find all the necessary information for the obituary. They wonder who to call to preside at the funeral, as well as other items like insurance policies, burial details, pallbearers, and a myriad of other details. By writing down their preferences and collecting all the important documents the dying can lighten the burden of the survivors. Here is Delores Bius' story of her stepmother who lightened their burden.

When Dad and I left the hospital in Florida shortly after my stepmother's death, we knew that taking care of the financial details during the following days and months would be painful and complicated.

When Dad went to their file cabinet after the funeral, one drawer contained all the documents he needed. They were labeled plainly and filed neatly in individual folders. My stepmother, Mary, had everything in order and easily located.

During the weeks that followed Dad commented several times about her thoughtfulness in making things easier for the survivor. "She epitomized the truth in I Corinthians 14:40, 'Let everything be done decently and in order,'" he shared.

Mary had handled most of their financial affairs. She had their financial assets listed for Dad to see at a glance. In her will she had instructions about the clothes she wanted to be dressed in at her funeral and where they could be found. She even specified the hymns to be sung.

She also provided a list of her most cherished possessions and their dispositions. She left me her set of English Wedgewood china. She left her huge collection of dolls to my sister, who is also a doll collector, with instructions to keep the ones she wanted and donate the rest to a children's home.

Among her possessions was a videotape of an awards banquet. The Chamber of Commerce had given it in honor of Mary six years earlier. She had served as President of the Chamber in that retirement community for twelve years. As a volunteer she had donated countless hours helping feed the poor, assisting well-baby clinics, and serving tirelessly in various charities.

The videotape showed her in glowing health, before she became seriously ill. What a wonderful keepsake. She left the original for Dad and had copies made for my sister and me.

Mary didn't forget her many friends either. She left a list of jewelry and figurines for them as keepsakes.

Realizing that Dad would probably appreciate having fewer knickknacks around the house to dust, she left instructions for him to have a garage sale and get rid of many of them.

When I returned to my home in Chicago, I decided to follow my stepmother's example. My husband and I already had wills drawn up, but I found most of our important papers dumped in the bottom drawer of a file cabinet.

I immediately began putting the documents in order, I made separate, labeled files for our life insurance, automobile insurance, real-estate records, retirement accounts, stocks, wills, and income-tax returns.

I tracked down our birth certificates, our marriage license, and my husband's army discharge papers and put them in a file folder labeled "Important Documents."

Last, but certainly not least, I made a list of all our assets. On another sheet I put down detailed instructions for my funeral arrangements and the disposition of items not mentioned in our wills.

I now had our affairs in order. It felt reassuring to know that if I should die, my remaining loved ones would not have to fret trying to find important papers and understand them. I even showed the drawer containing the files to my oldest son who is the executor of our wills.

When the day comes that your survivors will need important information, they will rise up and call you blessed, if you have your records easy to find and in order.[113]

## Organizing the Loose Ends

There is only one person who can really tie up the loose ends — only you know what you really want. Walsh wrote about the personal quality of preparation,

> In preparations for death the loose ends could be far more personal (and in most cases will be), but there are also some very practical loose ends. For instance, we need to delegate responsibility to family and friends for the estate, to arrange for distribution of personal gifts and remembrances, and to select the person who we most trust and desire as executor.
>
> Each choice made will reveal both the character and the deepest priorities of the individual facing death. There is a very enriching and fruitful realism to be gained from this experience, a candor that will serve to enhance our knowledge of this dying person.[115]

The following personal diary, from *Being Prepared*[114] is one way to create a record of personal preferences for the funeral. It also serves as a guide for gathering the information needed upon death.

It covers *personal details* such as your full name, date and place of birth, occupation, marital status, spouse's name, parents' names, education, children's names, and church affiliation. The diary reminds you to locate and organize important documents such as: benefit information, fraternal, recognition you have received. In it you will create a list of those to contact upon your death, including their phone numbers. This is an important list when the survivors seek to contact everyone.

The important documents you should compile include: your will, cemetery deed, insurance policies, safety deposit box numbers and keys, bank account books, real estate deeds, birth and marriage certificates, and mortgage papers.

The personal diary also includes places for your funeral preplanning. In it you can list your funeral director and funeral home, and details about your pre-arranged funeral contract (if any). Your choices include a presiding minister and a location for your funeral — a funeral chapel or your local church. You may also list pallbearers and honorary pallbearers, special music and singers, your favorite Scriptures, poetry, and authors. You can note what clothes and jewelry you wish to wear, as well as your choice of institutions for memorial gifts to go to.

There is also places to list your preferences for a casket\urn, burial vault, and flowers. If you have a family burial location you may list the details about number of spaces, which one is yours and which is for others.

## Personal Diary — Sheet One

# To My Family and Friends

After careful thought, I have completed this diary with specific information which may be helpful at the time of my death. I have expressed my preferences on a variety of subjects pertaining to my funeral which, unless changed by unexpected circumstances, I hereby desire and request.

_____
Signed

_____
Date

**Please note:** Do not place this personal diary in a safety deposit box as it may be sealed until *after* the funeral. Be sure to advise your family where it is kept.

EDUCATION                    ELEMENTARY
_____
                             HIGH SCHOOL
_____
                             COLLEGE
_____

RELIGIOUS AFFILIATION
NAMES OF CHILDREN:
_____

NAME            CITY   STATE   TELEPHONE
_____
_____
_____

## Personal Information—Myself

NAME:
_____
FIRST          MIDDLE         LAST

_____
ADDRESS              STREET

_____
CITY            STATE      ZIP

_____
TELEPHONE

_____
RESIDENT SINCE

_____
DATE OF BIRTH   MONTH    DAY    YEAR

_____
PLACE OF BIRTH    CITY  COUNTY  STATE

_____
OCCUPATION

_____
EMPLOYED BY OR RETIRED

_____
MARITAL STATUS

_____
NAME OF SPOUSE

_____
NAME OF FATHER      PLACE OF BIRTH   YEAR

_____
MOTHER'S MAIDEN NAME   PLACE OF BIRTH   YEAR

## Benefit Information:

_____
SOCIAL SECURITY NUMBER

_____
MILITARY SERVICE              BRANCH RANK

_____
DATE OF ENLISTMENT     DATE OF DISCHARGE

_____
SERIAL NUMBER

_____
FRATERNAL, SERVICE AND UNION MEMBERSHIPS
_____
_____

SPECIAL RECOGNITIONS:
_____

## Relatives and Friends to Notify:

NAME AND RELATIONSHIP  CITY STATE TELEPHONE
_____
_____
_____

147

# Personal Diary — Sheet Two

## Location of Important Documents:

HONORARY PALLBEARERS

WILL

CEMETERY DEED

INSURANCE POLICY/POLICIES

SPECIAL REQUESTS

SAFETY DEPOSIT BOX & KEYS

BANK ACCOUNTS

MUSIC, READINGS, ETC.

REAL ESTATE DEED(S)

BIRTH & MARRIAGE CERTIFICATES

CLOTHING, JEWELRY, ETC.

STOCKS AND BONDS

NEGOTIABLE PAPERS

MORTGAGE(S)

CASKET/URN

CONTRACTUAL AGREEMENTS

BURIAL VAULT

PROMISSORY NOTES

FLOWERS

OTHER

## Funeral Preferences:

## Family Burial Property:

LOCATION

FUNERAL DIRECTOR

NUMBER OF SPACES

FUNERAL HOME          ADDRESS          STATE

WHICH SPACE

PRE-ARRANGEMENT CONTRACT LOCATION

OTHER SPACES RESERVED FOR:

CLERGYMAN

LOCATION OF FUNERAL

PALLBEARERS

# One Last Testimony

No funeral can be more *personalized* than when it is planned by the deceased. For the Christian it is one last chance to comfort those who mourn, and to proclaim our victory in Christ.

Grief changes people.

If they let Him, God changes people . . .

Maybe through your funeral they will be *changed* by the grace and gospel of Christ. May they be changed by experiencing your assurance and hope in Christ through your favorite songs and hymns, your treasured Scriptures, and by listening to the retelling of *your* stories of faith and victory.

And when Jesus greets you He will say, "Well done, good and faithful servant. Enter in to the joy of your Lord."

# Notes

**Chapter 1**

1. Rich Mullins, "Land of My Sojourn," *A Liturgy, A Legacy & A Ragamuffin Band* (Nashville: Reunion Records, 1993).

2. Proverbs 12:25.

3. Granger E. Westberg, *Good Grief* (Philadelphia: Fortress Press, 1961, 1972), p. 9.

4. Doug Manning, *The Gift of Significance* (Hereford, TX: In-Sight Books, Inc., 1992), pp. 9-10.

5. C. S. Lewis, *A Grief Observed* (New York: Bantam Books, March 1976), pp. 10-11.

6. Kenn Filkins, *Comfort Those Who Mourn: How To Preach Personalized Funeral Messages* (Joplin, MO: College Press Publishing, 1993), pp. 38-39.

7. Manning, pp. 77-78.

8. James H. Horton and Francis Gretton, *Writing Incredibly Short, Plays, Poems, Stories* (New York: Harcourt Brace Jovanovich, Inc., 1972), p. 201.

9. Manning, p. 50.

**Chapter 2**

10. Manning, p. 44.

11. Ecclesiastes 3:1b, 2a, 4, 6a, 8a, NASB.

12. Diana J. McKendree, *The Spiral of Grief* (Evanston, IL: NSM Resources, Inc., 1989), p. 11.

13. Manning, p. 38.

14. Albert J.D. Walsh, *Reflections on Death and Grief* (Grand Rapids: Baker Book House, 1986), p. 79.

15. Lewis, p. 69.

16. C. Murray Parkes, "Effects of Bereavement on Physical and Mental Health — A Study of the Medical Records of Widows," *British Medical Journal* 2 (August 1964):274-279.

17. C. Murray Parkes, "The First Year of Bereavement," *Psychiatry* (November 1970):444-467.

18. Manning, pp. 39-40.

19. Delores Elaine Bius, "Life After Death — For The Survivor," *Live* (April 24, 1983), p. 3.

20. Westburg, p. 44.

21. Lewis, p. 67.

22. Westburg, pp. 48-49.

23. Manning, p. 74.

24. Westburg, pp. 31-32.

25. Lewis, p. 38.

26. Manning, p. 41.

27. Walsh, p. 65.

28. James C. Dobson, *Straight Talk* (Dallas: Word, Inc., 1991), [reprint March Letter, 1993, pp. 2-3].

29. Matthew 14:13.

30. Lois Duncan, "Funerals Are For The Living," *Woman's Day* (March 4th, 1986), p. 120.

## Chapter 3

31. Matthew 11:15.

32. Ecclesiastes 3:1a, 4, 5b, 7b, NASB.

33. Walsh, pp. 71-72.

34. Walsh, p. 22.

35. Psalm 6:6, NIV.

36. Manning, p. 36.

37. Walsh, p. 84.

38. Matthew 26:38b, 39b, NIV.

39. Walsh, p. 38.

40. Manning, pp. 13, 18.

41. Mark 9:1-10.

42. John 19:23-27.

43. John 19:28-29.

44. Luke 23:33-38.

45. Luke 23:39-43.

46. Matthew 27:45-46.

47. Matthew 27:46.

48. Luke 23:44-49.

49. John 19:30.

50. Delores Elaine Bius, "Coping With The Big 'C'," *Guide Magazine* (September 26, 1984), pp. 4-5.

51. Manning, p. 71.

52. Lewis, pp. 29-30.

53. Walsh, p. 49.

54. Manning, p. 52.

55. Delores Elaine Bius, "After The Funeral," *Home Life Magazine* (April, 1983), p. 22.

56. Manning, p. 52.


## Chapter 4

57. Lewis, p. 5.

58. *Ibid.*, p. 62.

59. Jon Tal Murphree, *A Loving God In A Suffering World* (Downers Grove: InterVarsity Press, 1981).

60. *Ibid.*, p. 113.

61. *Ibid.*, p. 41.

62. Acts 7:54-60.

63. Hebrews 11:33-34, 37.

64. Murphree, p. 47.


## Chapter 5

69. Psalm 6:6-7a.

70. David K. Switzer, *The Minister as Crisis Counselor* (Nashville: Abingdon Press, 1986), p. 154.

71. Westberg, p. 24.

72. *Michigan Funeral Facts* (Lansing, MI, 1993), p. 7.

73. Romans 1:18-32.

74. Walsh, p. 51.

75. Manning, p. 24.

76. Amy Hillyard Jensen, *Healing Grief* (Evanston, IL: Medic Publishing Co., 1980), p. 8.

77. Duncan, p. 120.

78. Jensen, p. 7.

79. Earl A. Grollman, *When Children Hurt* (Evanston, IL: NSM Resources, 1988), p. 4.

80. Duncan, p. 120.

**Chapter 6**

81. Duncan, p. 120.

82. McKendree, p. 17.

83. Manning, p. 22.

**Chapter 7**

84. Rich Mullins, "First Family," *Never Picture Perfect* (Nashville: Reunion Records, 1989).

85. Switzer, p. 147.

86. Marjorie Gordon, "The Grief Connection," *Christian Standard* (August 11, 1991), p. 8.

87. 2 Corinthians 1:4.

88. Switzer, p. 154.

89. Westberg, pp. 55-56.

90. Victor Parachin, "Suicide . . . ," *The Lookout* (May 3, 1992), p. 7.

91. Gordon, p. 8.

92. *Ibid.*, p. 9.

93. *Ibid.*

94. Manning, p. 88.

95. Elizabeth Richter, *Losing Someone You Love: When a Brother or Sister Dies* (New York: Putnam Publishing Group, 1986).

96. Mayo Mathers, "A Letter For Luke," *Focus On The Family* (November, 1991), p. 4.

97. Lewis, pp. 68-69.

98. Michael Bugeja, "Elegies in Appalachia," *Writer's Digest* (July, 1993), p. 12.

99. *Ibid.*, p. 16.

100. Delores Elaine Bius, "After The Funeral," *Home Life Magazine* (April, 1983), p. 22.

101. Herbert H. Wernecke, *When Loved Ones Are Called Home* (Grand Rapids: Baker Book House, 1972), pp. 33-34.

102. Charles Williams, "I Didn't Know Until . . . ," *NAFA Journal* (Volume 32, 1993) pp. 38-39.

**Chapter 8**

103. Psalm 23:4.

104. Walsh, p. 39.

105. Patricia Riesenweber, "Those Silent Moments," *Guidepost Magazine* (February, 1982), p. 36.

106. James C. Dobson, *Straight Talk* (Dallas: Word, Inc., 1991) [reprint March Letter, 1993, p. 3].

107. *Ibid.*

108. 2 Corinthians 4:16.

109. Wernecke, p. 19.

110. Walsh, p. 31.

111. Florence Littauer, *How To Get Along With Difficult People* (Eugene: Harvest House Publishers, 1984), pp. 162-163.

112. *Ibid.*, pp. 163-164.

113. Delores Elaine Bius, "Where Are Those Important Papers?" *Mature Living* (August, 1989), pp. 9-10.

114. *Being Prepared* (n.p.: M.K. Jones & Associates, Inc., 1988), pp. 12-15.

115. Walsh, p. 32.

# Bibliography

*Being Prepared.* N.p., M.K. Jones & Associates, Inc. 1988.

Filkins, Kenn. *Comfort Those Who Mourn: How To Preach Personalized Funeral Messages.* Joplin, MO: College Press Publishing, 1993.

Grollman, Earl A. *When Children Hurt.* Evanston, IL: NSM Resources, 1988.

Jensen, Amy Hillyard. *Healing Grief.* Evanston, IL: Medic Publishing Co., 1980.

Lewis, C.S. *A Grief Observed.* New York: Bantam Books, March, 1976.

Manning, Doug. *The Gift of Significance.* Hereford, TX: In-Sight Books, Inc., 1992.

McKendree, Diana J. *The Spiral Of Grief.* Evanston, IL: NSM Resources, Inc., 1989.

Murphree, Jon Tal. *A Loving God In A Suffering World.* Downers Grove: InterVarsity Press, 1981.

Richter, Elizabeth. *Losing Someone You Love: When a Brother or Sister Dies.* New York: Putnam Publishing Group, 1986.

Switzer, David K. *The Minister as Crisis Counselor.* Nashville: Abingdon Press, 1986.

Walsh, Albert J.D. *Reflections Of Death And Grief.* Grand Rapids: Baker Book House, 1986.

Wernecke, Herbert H. *When Loved Ones Are Called Home.* Grand Rapids: Baker Book House, 1972.

Westberg, Granger E. *Good Grief.* Philadelphia: Fortress Press, 1962.